W9-BYW-222

International Law in Archaic Rome

*Ancient Society and History*

# International Law in Archaic Rome

# ALAN WATSON

*War and Religion*

The Johns Hopkins University Press
Baltimore and London

© 1993 The Johns Hopkins University Press
All rights reserved
Printed in the United States of America on acid-free paper

The Johns Hopkins University Press
2715 North Charles Street
Baltimore, Maryland 21218-4319
The Johns Hopkins Press Ltd., London

Library of Congress Cataloging-in-Publication Data

Watson, Alan.
  International law in archaic Rome : war and religion / Alan
Watson.
     p.   cm. — (Ancient society and history)
  Includes bibliographical references (p.     ) and index.
  ISBN 0-8018-4506-8 (hc : acid-free paper)
  1. War (Roman law) 2. Rome—Foreign relations—Treaties.
3. Roman law—Religious aspects. 4. Fetiales. 5. International
law—Rome.   I. Title. II. Series.
KJA3320.W38   1993
341.6'0937—dc20                              92-20432

A catalog record for this book is available from the British Library.

*for Grandma,*
*Jean Bowen*

# Contents

# Contents

# Preface

This book has a strong, new thesis: that, in the stages leading up to a Roman declaration of war, which were cast in the form of a trial process, the gods were not called upon to be witnesses, as is always claimed, but to be judges. Accordingly, our picture of the responsible priests, the *fetiales,* and their law must be completely changed.

The book is very different from my previous one, *The State, Law and Religion: Pagan Rome.* Certainly both books deal with the same people, the Romans, and much the same historical period. Both concern the relationship between law, religion, and the state. But that earlier book dealt above all with the development of private law, the impact of the College of Pontiffs on secular law, and pontifical law. The development was internal, with considerable input from the political struggle between patricians and plebeians. The religion at issue concerned the right relations between deities and humans. The gods had to be appeased and served and persuaded to be favorable; or they might take revenge.

In this book the law is international, and local conflicts between the orders are not relevant. The focus is not on private law. Again, the deities do not appear this time as those who have suffered an injury or who will confer a favor. Instead they are the judges to legal disputes between peoples, or the avengers of broken faith in a treaty.

The judgment of the gods appears most clearly in the declaration of a war. That the war about to be waged is just is the legal verdict of the gods. So Roman international law in appearance (but not in actuality) is primarily a law of war.[1] In spirit it is also unlike much that is called international law as it existed from Roman times until 1919, when the Permanent International Court of Justice was set up by the Treaty of Versailles. Until that time there was seldom a system of arbiters with power to adjudicate in international disputes. In contrast, for the Romans the gods were the International Court of Justice: without judgments in a trial process there can be no law.[2] It is, of course, common to characterize a lawsuit as war, but rare to portray war as a lawsuit.[3] The system strikes a remarkably contemporary note. The insistence that the gods first judge a war to be just before the Romans declare it brings sharply to mind President Bush seeking United Nations' approval before the Gulf War.

The scope of the book should be noted. It is about international relations enshrined in law and religion; that is, it concerns the sphere of operations of these Roman priests known as *fetiales*. Because the fetial ritual early lost most of its force, the focus of the book is on early Rome.[4] It does not directly concern the operations of these other priests, the *pontifices*. Certainly the *pontifices* were responsible for the correct formulation of prayers and vows in war as in peace. But these prayers and vows are not part of international relations: they are between the Romans and their gods. Nor does it concern *postliminium*, basically the recovery of certain legal rights by a Roman who had been taken prisoner by the enemy and who returned home without dishonor. *Postliminium* is simply part of internal Roman private law.

A matter of dispute is the trustworthiness of sources for early Roman history. I have argued elsewhere that they do, in general, represent faithfully archaic law and religion.[5] In this instance, we can have great faith in the veracity of the sources, because in the main we are concerned not with particular historical events, but with the procedures and formulation of treaties and declarations of war. As Georges Dumézil insists, we are dealing with "formulas used by competent specialist priests every time there was a need for them."[6] As such they would remain in the memory, and they could not be invented subsequently for a particular propaganda reason. Moreover, if when we leave aside the issue of the veracity of the sources the texts tell a consistent and plausible story, then, *on that topic,* the story is the best argument for the accuracy of the sources. I hope I will provide such a plausible story for the early history of the *ius fetiale.* The reliability or otherwise of the sources cannot be established in the abstract but only in light of the story they tell.

The Romans were the most legalistic of all peoples, and their system of private law is their greatest intellectual achievement, and their greatest gift to subsequent ages. This law is remarkably secular. Until the very late Republic, the Romans regarded themselves, and were regarded by others, as the most religious people. Their state religion is primarily legalistic, much more concerned with formalities and observances than with beliefs or personal piety. At the same time, the Romans were the most successfully imperialistic people in antiquity, with an economy in the Republic resting on conquest and slavery. The Romans in the Republic attributed their success in war to their piety. Among my aims for this book is a resolution of at least some of the apparent paradoxes in this paragraph.[7]

# Acknowledgments

This book developed from a suggestion by my friend and colleague, Peter Hoffer, that I write on the Roman law of war. He put me further in his debt by reading the manuscript and giving me copious criticisms. Similar debts were incurred to John Cairns and Olivia Robinson. Jerzy Linderski, who has a unique grasp of Roman history, law, and religion, read the book for the Johns Hopkins University Press. His acute criticisms have, not for the first time, saved me from grievous error.

The staff of the University of Georgia Law Library was unfailingly helpful, and skilled at finding scarce material for me. Professor Hans Ankum, of the University of Amsterdam, and Professor Dieter Nörr, of the University of Munich, provided me with material not easily available in this country on interlibrary loan. As before, Karen Bramlett was the perfect secretary.

Translations from Greek are taken from those in the Loeb Classical Library, with occasional modifications.

# Abbreviations

| | |
|---|---|
| Catalano, *Linee*, 1 | P. Catalano, *Linee del sistema sovrana-zionale romano*, vol. 1 (Turin, 1965) |
| D | *Digestum Justiniani* |
| Dumézil, *Archaic Religion*, 1, 2 | G. Dumézil, *Archaic Roman Religion*, vols. 1, 2 (Chicago, 1970) |
| G | *Gai Institutiones* |
| J | *Justiniani Institutiones* |
| Kaser, *Zivilprozessrecht* | Max Kaser, *Das römische Zivilprozess-recht* (Munich, 1966) |
| Latte, *Religionsgeschichte* | K. Latte, *Römische Religionsgeschichte*, 2nd ed. (Munich, 1907) |
| Michel, "Extradition" | J.-H. Michel, "L'extradition du général en droit romain," *Latomus* 39 (1980): 675ff. |

Nörr, *Aspekte*      D. Nörr, *Aspekte des römischen Völker-rechts; Die Bronzetafel von Alcántara* (Munich, 1989)

Ogilvie, *Livy*      R. M. Ogilvie, *A Commentary on Livy, Books 1–5* (Oxford, 1965)

Paradisi, "Due aspetti"      B. Paradisi, "Due aspetti fondamentali nella formazione del diritto internazionale antico," *Annali di Storia del Diritto* 1 (1957): 169ff.

RE      *Paulys Real-Encyclopädie der klassischen Altertumswissenschaft,* ed. G. Wissowa et al. (Stuttgart, 1973–)

Saulnier, "Rôle"      C. Saulnier, "Le rôle des prêtres fétiaux et l'application du "ius fetiale" à Rome," *Revue historique du droit français et étranger* 58 (1980): 171ff.

Thomas, *Textbook*      J. A. C. Thomas, *Textbook of Roman Law* (Amsterdam, 1970)

Watson, *State, Law and Religion*      A. Watson, *The State, Law and Religion: Pagan Rome* (Athens, Ga., 1992).

Wieacker, *Rechtsgeschichte,* 1      F. Wieacker, *Römische Rechtsgeschichte,* vol. 1 (Munich, 1988)

Wissowa, *Religion und Kultus*      G. Wissowa, *Religion und Kultus der Römer,* 2nd ed. (Munich, 1912)

Ziegler, "Völkerrecht"      K.-H. Ziegler, "Das Völkerrecht der römischen Republik," in *Aufstieg und Niedergang der römischen Welt,* vol. 1, ed. H. Temporini (Berlin, 1972), pp. 68ff.

# One

# The *Fetiales*

W ith the exception of the *flamines*, the priests of the Roman state religion were not in the service of any particular deity. They were organized in colleges or sodalities and charged with set functions. Thus, the *pontifices* originally were an advisory board to assist the kings, then other leading officials, with their sacred functions. At all times their main responsibility was to keep the Roman state in the right relationship with the gods. The *augures*, on the other hand, were charged with interpreting the auspices.

The *fetiales*,[1] with whom we will be concerned in this volume, formed one of the oldest Roman priestly sodalities, ranking in dignity after only the College of Pontiffs and College of Augurs and the later College of Septemviri Epulonum.[2] They were the priests responsible for the proper, religious conduct of international relations, including the observance of the sacred forms.[3] Ancient writers are unanimous that the *fetiales* were introduced in the regal period (which traditionally runs from 753 to 509 B.C.), though the sources disagree as to which king was responsible.[4] Some of these texts deserve to be quoted in full at the outset (and not paraphrased) since they also provide us with the best outline of the fetials' nature and function.

Dionysius of Halicarnassus gives the credit to Numa, the second king who, according to tradition, ruled from 715 to 673 B.C.

2.72. The seventh division of his sacred institutions was devoted to the college of the *fetiales;* these may be called in Greek *eirênodikai* or "arbiters of peace." They are chosen men, from the best families, and exercise their holy office for life; King Numa was also the first who instituted this holy magistracy among the Romans. 2. But whether he took his example from those called the Aequicoli, according to the opinion of some, or from the city of Ardea, as Gellius writes, I cannot say. It is sufficient for me to state that before Numa's reign the college of the *fetiales* did not exist among the Romans. 3. It was instituted by Numa when he was upon the point of making war on the people of Fidenae, who had raided and ravaged his territories, in order to see whether they would come to an accommodation with him without war; and that is what they actually did, being constrained by necessity. But since the college of the *fetiales* is not in use among the Greeks, I think it incumbent on me to relate how many and how great affairs fall under its jurisdiction, to the end that those who are unacquainted with the piety practiced by the Romans of those times may not be surprised to find that all their wars had the most successful outcome; 4. for it will appear that the origins and motives of them all were most holy, and for this reason especially the gods were propitious to them in the dangers that attended them. The multitude of duties, to be sure, that fall within the province of these *fetiales* make it no easy matter to enumerate them all; but to indicate them by a summary outline, they are as follows: 5. It is their duty to take care that the Romans do not enter upon an unjust war against any city in alliance with them, and if others begin the violation of treaties against them, to go as ambassadors and first make formal demand for justice, and then, if the others refuse to comply with their demands, to sanction war. In like manner, if any people in alliance with the Romans complain of having been injured by them and demand justice, these men are to determine whether they have suffered anything in violation of their alliance; and if they find their complaints well grounded, they are to seize the accused and deliver them up to the injured parties. They are also to take cognizance of the crimes committed against ambassadors, to take care that treaties are religiously observed, to make peace, and if they find that peace has been made otherwise than is prescribed by the holy laws, to set it aside; and to inquire into and expiate the transgressions of the generals in so far as they relate to oaths and treaties, concerning which I shall speak in the proper places. 6. As to the functions they performed in the quality of heralds when they went to demand justice of any city thought to have injured the Romans (for these things also are worthy of our knowledge, since they were carried out with great regard to both religion and justice), I have received the following account: One of these *fetiales,* chosen by his colleagues, wearing his sacred robes and insignia to distinguish him from all others, proceeded towards the city whose inhabitants had done the injury; and, stopping at the border, he called upon Jupiter and the rest of the gods to witness that he was come to demand justice on behalf of the Roman State. 7. Thereupon he took an oath that he was going to a city that had done an injury; and having uttered the most dreadful imprecations against himself and Rome, if what he averred was not true, he then entered their borders. Afterwards, he called to witness the first person he met, whether it was one of the countrymen or one of the townspeople, and having repeated the same imprecations, he advanced towards the city. And before he entered it he called to witness in the same manner the gate-keeper or the first person he met at the gates, after which he proceeded to the forum; and taking his stand there, he discussed with the magistrates the reasons for his coming, adding everywhere the same oaths and imprecations. 8. If, then, they were disposed to offer satisfaction by delivering up the guilty, he departed as a friend, taking leave of friends, carrying the prisoners with him. Or, if they desired time to deliberate, he allowed them ten days, after which he returned and waited till they had made this request three times. But after the expiration of the thirty days, if the city still persisted in refusing to grant him justice, he called both the celestial and infernal gods to witness and went away, saying no more than this, that the Roman State would deliberate at its leisure concerning these people. 9. Afterwards he, together with the other *fetiales,* appeared before the senate and declared that they had done everything that was ordained by the holy laws, and that, if the senators wished to vote for war, there would be no obstacle on the part of the gods. But if any of these things was omitted, neither the senate nor the people had the power to vote for war. Such, then, is the account we have received concerning the *fetiales.*

This text is the best introduction to the *fetiales.* It summarizes all of their functions. The fetials have to supervise the steps leading to a declaration of war: they have to ensure that the Romans do not declare an unjust war; ask for justice from a people in breach of an obligation before they decide for war; decide whether restitution and surrender of wrongdoers should be made to or by the Romans; declare war; and make peace and treaties.

A striking feature of the text and others is that it represents the *fetiales* as an artificial creation. They were not part of the original, organic, religious system of Rome. It should also be noted at this stage that Dionysius emphasizes that there was no equivalent body of priests among the Greeks.

Plutarch makes the same identification of the creator of the priesthood at Rome:

> *Numa,* 12.3. Numa also established many other orders of priesthood, of which I shall mention two besides, those of the Salii and the *fetiales,* which more than any others give evidence of the man's reverent piety. The *fetiales* were guardians of peace, so to speak, and in my opinion took their name from their office, which was to put a stop to disputes by oral conference, or *parley;* and they would not suffer a hostile expedition to be made before any hope of getting justice had been cut off. 4. For the Greeks call it peace when two parties settle their quarrels by mutual conference, and not by violence. And the Roman *fetiales* often went to those who were doing them a wrong and made personal appeals for fair treatment; but if the unfair treatment continued, they called the gods to witness, invoked many dreadful evils upon themselves and their country in case they resorted to hostilities unjustly, and so declared war upon them. 5. But if they forbade it or withheld their consent, neither soldier nor king of Rome could lawfully take up arms. War had to begin with their verdict that it was just, and the ruler, on receiving this verdict, must then deliberate on the proper way to wage it. And it is said that the dreadful disaster which the city experienced at the hands of the Gauls was in consequence of the illegal treatment of these priests.
>
> 6. For when the barbarians were besieging Clusium, Fabius Ambustus was sent from Rome to their camp to bring about a cessation of hostilities on behalf of the besieged. But on receiving an unseemly answer, he thought his office of ambassador was at an end, and committed the youthful folly of taking up arms for the Clusians and challenging the bravest of the barbarians to single combat. Fabius fought successfully, unhorsed his adversary, and stripped him of his armour. 7. But

when the Gauls discovered who he was, they sent a herald to Rome denouncing Fabius for violating a truce, breaking his oath, and fighting against them before war was formally declared. At Rome the *fetiales* tried to persuade the senate to deliver Fabius into the hands of the Gauls, but he took refuge with the multitude, and through the favor of the populace evaded his punishment. After a little, therefore, the Gauls came up and sacked Rome, with the exception of the Capitol. But this story is more fully given in my life of Camillus.[5]

Cicero, however, prefers to nominate as originator of the fetials Tullus Hostilius, Numa's successor, who is supposed to have reigned from 673 to 642:

De re publica, 2.17.31. After the death of king Pompilius [Numa] the people created Tullus Hostilius king in the *comitia curiata,* the interrex putting the question, and he followed the example of Pompilius and consulted the people in the *comitia curiata* as to his royal powers. He excelled in military skill and glory, and was responsible for great deeds of war. From his spoils he built and walled in a meeting hall for an assembly of the people, and for the senate; and he formulated the legal rules by which wars might be declared. These rules, which he had so justly created, he consecrated with fetial rites so that every war that had not been declared and announced should be judged to be unjust and impious.[6]

Tullius's successor, Ancus Marcius (640–616 B.C.), is the choice of the grammarian Servius,[7] of Aurelius Victor,[8] and also, apparently, of Livy. Thus:

Servius, In Vergilii Aeneidon libris 10.14. . . . THEN IT WILL BE PERMITTED TO RAVAGE: to make *clarigatio* [a solemn demand for redress], that is, to declare war through the *fetiales*. For Ancus Marcius, when he saw the Roman people burning with love of wars, and generally to wage war on peoples with no just reason and thus dangers were created, sent to the Aequicoli and took over the fetial law by which war was declared in this way, just as Livy reports about the Albans. For if ever men or animals were seized from the Roman people by any nation, then with the fetials (that is the priests charged with making treaties) went also the *pater patratus,* and standing before the boundaries declared the cause of the war in a clear voice, and if they refused to restore the property that had been seized or hand over the authors of insult, he threw the spear, which was the beginning of the fight, and then it was permitted by the custom of war to seize property. *Clarigatio* was so called either from the clear voice [*clara voce*] which the *pater patratus* used, or from χλήρῳ that is, by chance: for they invaded the fields of the enemy by chance: hence those who by law share out the goods of the deceased are called χληρονόμοι in Greek.[9]

Livy, 1.32.5. In order, however, since Numa had established religious rites in peace time, that ceremonials might be instituted for war, and that wars might not only be waged, but even declared by some ritual, he [Ancus] copied down from the ancient tribe of the Aequicoli the law that the fetials now have, by which redress is demanded.[10]

As we have already seen, the Romans were not the only people to have *fetiales*. They are found also among Latin peoples,[11] such as those from Ardea[12] and Lavinium,[13] and the Albans.[14] They are also found among some non-Latin people of central Italy, such as the Falisci, from whom Servius in another text says the Romans took them.[15] The Falisci, though not Etruscan and of uncertain origin, inhabited Etruria. Their language was latinate, and their religion was basically similar to that of the Latins and Sabines (though influenced by the Etruscans).[16] The account of Servius here is rather odd since he links the borrowing of the *ius fetiale* from the Faliscans with the making of the Twelve Tables:

In Vergilii Aeneidon libris 7.695. . . . But he calls the Faliscans just, because the Roman people who had sent ten men took from them the fetial law and some supplements to the Twelve Tables which it had from the Athenians.[17]

But the Twelve Tables seem to date from the middle of the fifth century B.C., which is much too late for the introduction of the *ius fetiale* to Rome.[18] Perhaps the dating is wrong, or (if we give any credence to the text) the text is an indication of some surprise that the Faliscans, a non-Latin people, had a fetial law (at least from the fifth century B.C.) Again, a strong tradition, including the text first quoted from Servius, claims that the fetials were the creation of Fertor Resius, king of the Aequicoli, and that the Romans took them from them.[19] The Aequicoli may have been Oscans or Volsci, and were major enemies of the Romans in the fifth century B.C.

The linking of the Aequicoli with the *ius fetiale* may well be, as has been suggested, the result of an etymological game: 'Aequicoli' means 'cultivators of justice'.[20] Another tradition was that the Romans took the fetials from Latin Ardea.[21] The strong probability is that the *ius fetiale* was a Latin rite—the Latins had other religious institutions in common, and it was also adopted for convenience by a few neighbors.

There is no evidence of *fetiales* beyond central Italy or, indeed, among the Etruscans.[22] The matter is important because the Roman law of war and treaties originally required reciprocal behavior by the *fetiales* of the other people. Thus, the Roman law of war and treaties was created for dealings with other central Italian, particularly Latin, peoples. Its history is the story of its disintegration as Rome expanded from its narrow beginnings.

There is, however, general agreement among modern scholars that the *ius fetiale* was not introduced into Rome by one of the kings but existed even before the city was founded.[23] Part of the argument is that the sacrifice of a pig by using a stone knife, and casting a spear with a fire-hardened tip, point to the Neolithic period and not to a time when bronze would have been used for weapons and implements.[24] A more important argument adduced is this very shared tradition of the *fetiales* with other Latins. This points to the common heritage that is seen in other religious rituals, especially that of Juppiter Feretrius near Alba Longa, of Diana at Lake Nemi, and of Venus at Lavinium.[25] There is also, it is observed, the Feriae Latinae during which warfare was forbidden.[26] This general agreement, however, requires qualification. Certainly, the fetial rite is very ancient but the whole functions of the *fetiales* relate to declarations of war, treaty making, and the surrender of wrongdoers, and nothing more. The forms, in their pristine state, require reciprocal handling by other fetials. That is to say that the *ius fetiale* must date back to a time when the Latin communities were separate—only then could there be two sides. They are, thus, not an element dating from forever among the Latins, but a subsequent, deliberate creation with the precise function of keeping peace among the Latins and some of their neighbors. Dionysius of Halicarnassus and Plutarch are right to stress that the *fetiales* have, above all, a function relating to peace, not war. Fetial law may well have existed before Rome, and go back to the Stone Age. But it came into being only after the Latins split into separate communities.

Viewed from this perspective we can also see that a question raised by Kurt Latte is unreal, namely whether war was always excluded between the members of the Latin League, and the prohibition on war during the Feriae Latinae related to external war. The pure form of the *ius fetiale* regarded only relations, including war, among the Latins; hence war between members of the Latin League was not thought of as excluded.

The fetial college at Rome[27] contained twenty members[28] who were chosen by cooptation for life.[29] Originally they had to be patricians—that restriction, which applied to Roman priests generally, was only removed by the *lex Ogulnia* of 300 B.C. Even later, the *collegium* contained the leading men of the state. Thus, Aulus Cornelius Arvina, the fetial named by Livy, 9.10.8, was the Roman dictator two years earlier, in 322,[30] and consul twice before that.[31] Inscriptions identify fetials as high public magistrates such as consul, proconsul, or quaestor.[32] The emperor Augustus was a fetial,[33] as was Claudius,[34] and, apparently, Marcus Aurelius.[35] Like other priests, they were exempt from military service and were priests only part-time.[36]

For the preliminary steps in dealings with another people we have information from Livy relating to the reign of Tullus Hostilius:

1.24.3. . . . Different treaties have different provisions, but all are made in the same way. 4. On the present occasion we are told they acted as follows, and there is no record of any older treaty. The fetial asked King Tullus: "Do you command me, king, to strike a treaty with the *pater patratus* of the Alban people." Being so commanded by the king, he said, "I ask you for the sacred herb." 5. The king said "Take it uncontaminated." The fetial brought from the citadel an uncontaminated plant. After this he asked the king, "King, do you make me the royal messenger of the Roman people of the Quirites, with my emblems and my companions?" The king replied, "So far as may be done without fraud of mine and of the Roman people of the Quirites, I grant it." 6. The fetial was Marcus Valerius. He made Spurius Fusius the *pater patratus,* touching his head and hair with the leafy twig. The *pater patratus* is appointed to pronounce the oath, that is to consecrate the treaty; and this he does with many words, recited in a long metrical form which is not worthwhile to repeat.[37]

Although the text relates to the preparations for making a treaty, we may assume that the early steps for declaring a war were similar.

How the fetial who addressed the king was chosen we do not know. He was called the *verbenarius* because the twig or herb that he collected was called *verbena.* What this was cannot be identified, though Servius considered it was rosemary or frankincense taken from the Capitol, and he also says the term was used wrongly for all sacred plants such as a twig of laurel, olive, or myrtle.[38] Pliny the Elder considered it a plant pulled from the citadel, retaining its earth.[39] The *verbena* was regarded as a symbol of peace.[40] Indeed, in the passages quoted previously from Dionysius of Halicarnassus and Plutarch, the main function of the fetials was stated to be to keep peace.[41]

The main deity for the *fetiales* was Jupiter, Juppiter Lapis and Juppiter Feretrius, so the *verbena* was plucked from the citadel (*arx*) which was a cult spot for Jupiter, the most important of the Roman gods.[42] From the holy place of Juppiter Feretrius they also took the symbols of their office, the scepter and stone of flint.[43]

The *verbenarius* chose the *pater patratus* from among the other fetials, and he was the real spokesman for the Roman people. The significance of the title is not known.[44] The *pater patratus* carried the scepter (which Servius says was in place of an image of Jupiter) and stone of flint.[45] He wore priestly garments,[46] which had to be of wool,[47] and his head was covered with a woolen cap.[48]

The procedures once the *verbenarius* and the *pater patratus* reached the boundaries of the other people will be discussed in subsequent chapters.[49]

# Two

## *Testis*, Witness:
## *Testis*, Judge

A
s is well known, Roman declarations of war were cast in the form of the proceedings of a trial process.[1] The forms and legal aspects of declarations of war are the subject matter of chapter 3. This chapter will deal with only one detail of such declarations of war, which must be treated first because it is vital and it has been misunderstood. The detail is, however, fundamental not only for an understanding of declarations of war but also for the early form of civil proceedings known as *legis actiones*. Even more important, as will emerge, the detail is fundamental for the whole relationship of the Romans to their deities.

A standard translation of the relevant part of the formulation of a declaration of war in Livy, 1.32.10, would be:

> "Hear, Jupiter, and thou Janus Quirinus, and hear all heavenly gods, and ye, gods of earth, and ye of the lower world; I call you to witness that this people"—naming whatever people it is—"is unjust, and does not make just reparation. But of these matters we will take counsel of the elders in our country, how we may obtain our right."[2]

According to this translation, the gods are called to witness.[3] Max Kaser clarifies the nature of witnessing thus:

> The "witnessing" that the gods should perform means that they, in the war about to begin with the agreement of the senate, destroy the "unjust" enemy people and provide a just Roman victory. This calling upon the gods, too, is an oath: it pledges the Roman people to the gods for the truth of the claim against the opponents for their express unjust declaration and seeks thus to obtain their support.[4]

This approach, I believe, is mistaken. There is no oath in this part of the formulation, and no pledge to the gods for the truth of the Roman claim. There is also no sign of seeking the support of the gods. Nor are the gods asked to destroy the enemy. Above all, I believe, the words *Ego vos testor* should not be taken to mean "I call you to be witnesses," but "I call you to be judges."[5] The fundamental error on this last point has caused this text (and others) to be obviously misread in other regards.

Of course, in classical Latin, *testes* means 'witnesses' and *testari* 'to bear witness'. But that need not have been the original or sole meaning. *Testis* (from which *testari* is formed) is derived from a root signifying 'a third person'.[6] But if the parties to a lawsuit are the first and second persons, then who is the third person? On a priori grounds it is just as likely to be the judge as a witness. Moreover, if one felt that, because of the subsequent meaning of *testis,* an original part (at least) of its general connotation must have included 'witness', then it could be claimed that in one sense a judge is a witness. He attests that the trial is properly carried out and is in accord with whatever "facts" are considered relevant. From the etymology I want to claim only that 'judge' cannot be excluded as the original or part of the original meaning of *testis*. I am not asserting that it proves *testis* originally meant 'judge'.

But then there are general and particular considerations that make it necessary to hold that in the Roman declarations of war the gods were, indeed, called upon to be judges.

The general considerations are that, as has long been recognized, declarations of war are cast in the form of a lawsuit, and there can be no lawsuit without a judge or judges. There can also be no witnesses in a trial if there is no judge to hear them. In a lawsuit, judges are logically prior to witnesses. Again, of necessity, there have to be judges, but no other possible candidates for the post are mentioned or can be imagined. Indeed, in an international dispute treated as a legal process, when there is no body akin in authority to the International Court and no mutually appointed arbiter, the only possible judges are the gods.

The particular consideration comes from Livy's description of an earlier stage in the formalities for the declaration of war:

> 1.32.6. When the envoy reaches the boundaries of the people from whom restitution is sought, he covers his head with a cap, the covering is of wool, and he says, "Hear Jupiter; hear you boundaries"—he names of which people—"Let righteousness hear. I am the public messenger of the Roman people. Duly and righteously commissioned, I come. Let faith be given to my words." He recites his demands. 7. Then he makes Jupiter *testis:* "If I wrongfully and contrary to religion demand that those men and those things be surrendered to me, then let me never enjoy my native land."[7]

The fetial calls upon Jupiter, the opponent's boundaries, and *fas,* to hear him, but he makes only Jupiter *testis.* In this context, 'witness' is thus clearly an inappropriate translation. 'Witness' would fit all three—Jupiter, the boundaries, and *fas.* Moreover, as *testis,* Jupiter is asked to do more than witness: he is to act. *Testis* appears here in Livy's account of the proceedings, and not as if it were in the direct speech of the *pater patratus.* But Livy is reporting the standard formulation. It is to be observed that elsewhere in book 1 Livy uses other words in an archaic sense that he is likely to have found in his sources. Thus, *emere* long before his time meant 'to purchase', but in older Latin it meant simply 'to take'.[8] Thus, at 1.12.4 Livy has "Arcem iam scelere emptam Sabini habent," and this can only mean "The Sabines already hold the fortress, taken by a crime," and not "bought by a crime." Of course, I leave open the question whether Livy used *testis* to mean 'judge' or was simply following the traditional language with no understanding of the original meaning. It is not difficult to imagine that, once the primary meaning of *testis* had become 'witness', the fetials' declaration would be misunderstood.[9]

Again, in the rather different formulaic context of Livy, 1.22.7, *testes* means 'judges', not 'witnesses'.

To this Tullus replied: "Tell your king that the Roman king makes the gods *testes* as to which people spurned and dismissed the envoys seeking redress, that they may call down all the disasters of this war upon that people."[10]

In this declaration, "ut in eum omnes expetant huiusce clades belli," the verb *expetant* is plural, "that they may call down" and the only possible plural subject is *dei* 'gods', since both king and people are singular. Here it is self-evident in the words of Tullus that the gods are not being asked to be witnesses. Again, the gods are to act, and to punish. They are judges in a criminal suit, not witnesses.

It is worth stressing that the scholarly acceptance without question that in the context of the fetials, as in others, *testis* had the sense of 'witness' meant that no other possibility has hitherto (to my knowledge) been considered. The question who was to be the judge (or judges) in this lawsuit has not been raised, and the exact role envisaged for Jupiter (and other gods) has not been investigated. The strength of the case for the god (or the gods) sitting in judgment has simply been overlooked.

The formulations we have seen in this chapter, it should be stressed, are very different from what we find in Roman prayers and vows. There is no asking here for the gods to favor or intercede for the Romans. There is no promise to do something in return for a favor from the gods. Rather, the call is simply to the gods to judge whose claim is just. Naturally, the Roman claimants believe or expect that it is they who make just demands, but they do not request preferential treatment.

The meaning of *testes* 'judges' in fetial law also casts light on the meaning of *litis contestatio* in Roman procedure. Surprisingly, perhaps, on this point we have more textual guidance for fetial law than for the *legis actiones*. *Contestatio* is a word formed from *testis* and, indeed, in the sources *litis contestatio* occurs, we are told, when the parties say *testes estote*. Speaking generally, *litis contestatio* is the point of no return in a lawsuit. After its occurrence, if the plaintiff stops his action, he cannot bring another on the same basis. We need not concern ourselves with its theoretical grounding (which is much disputed), such as whether the basis of jurisdiction was the agreement of the parties, and hence the acceptance of jurisdiction (at the moment of *litis contestatio*) was akin to a contract that replaced the preceding obligation.[11]

Any light that may be shed on procedure will be on the archaic *legis actio* rather than on the later republican and classical *formula*. A first reason for this claim is that the fetials' formulations correspond in form to the *legis actio*, not to the *formula*. Second, the *legis actio* corresponds to the fetials' formulations in point of date. Third, *testes estote* is known only for *legis actiones*; and only there is there scope for such a formal exclamation by the parties.

Two preliminary points on the *legis actio* system should be mentioned. First, the procedure (as also in the formulary system) was in two stages: a formal stage in front of a magistrate, particularly characteristic of the *legis actio*; and, if all the conditions for an action were present, a second informal stage before a judge or judges.[12] The whole point of this first stage was to determine whether there was in appearance the requisites for a trial process and to fix the parameters of the trial. *Litis contestatio* occurred at the very end of these proceedings before the magistrate. The second preliminary point is that (as also in the formulary system) the parties, not the magistrate, chose the judge or judges.[13]

To set the scene for the nature of *litis contestatio* and the sources for it, we may quote again Max Kaser:

> With this formal act, through the working together of the parties and the praeter, is founded the *lis*, the legal dispute, that is to say the settling, in accordance with its basis and contents, of the terms of the legal claim of the plaintiff that is disputed by the defendant. In this act we see the *litis contestatio* which is so named because witnesses are called to this important proceeding. [Here Kaser inserts the footnote about to be mentioned.] With this act the parties submit themselves to the process, in which the legal question disputed by them will be decided in a way that is binding upon them.[14]

In a note to this passage, Kaser quotes the sole two passages, both from Festus, which are directly relevant. Sextus Pompeius Festus of the late second century A.D. epitomized *De significatu verborum*

("On the Meaning of Words") of the scholar Verrius Flaccus of the Augustan age. Neither Festus nor Verrius Flaccus was a jurist.

> Festus, s.v. *contestari litem*. Two or more adversaries are said to *contestari* the law suit because, when the conditions for a trial are fulfilled,[15] either of the parties is accustomed to say: *testes estote*.[16]
>
> s.v. *contestari*. *Contestari* is when either party to a law suit says: *testes estote*.[17]

For Kaser and (to the best of my knowledge) all other scholars,[18] the words in these passages, *testes estote,* which bring about the fateful *litis contestatio,* mean 'be witnesses'. For me, they mean 'be judges'.

For my position I would urge the following arguments. First, of course, in the analogous declarations by the fetials, *testes* must mean 'judges'. Second, it would be surprising if persons were called to be witnesses at this, the concluding act, of the formal proceedings before the magistrate, rather than at the second stage, before the judges. Third, the moment of declaration "Be witnesses" scarcely seems able to bear the weight of the momentous *litis contestatio*.[19] The appointment of judges on the other hand is precisely fitting for the conclusion of the formal proceedings before the magistrate. And we know that in early law the parties appointed the judges at once.[20] Fourth, otherwise we have no evidence of how the judge was appointed in the early *legis actio.*

Thus, *litis contestatio* would mean 'the call to act as judges' " rather than 'the plea to act as witnesses'.

For this explanation it is not necessary that the words *testes estote* occurred in every type of *legis actio.* The term *litis contestatio* could have originated to designate this decisive moment if *testes estote* marked the climax of either the oldest or the most important of the *legis actiones.* The *legis actio sacramento* is usually held to be both the oldest, with ancient roots,[21] and the most important because it could be used whenever a legal situation had not been provided with some other form.[22] *Testes estote* would fit perfectly after the challenge to the oath.[23]

*Testes estote* would cease to be relevant wording in the formal part of the *legis actio sacramento* after the passing of the *lex Pinaria,* which enacted that the judge was to be chosen thirty days after these proceedings *in iure*.[24] The dating of the *lex Pinaria* is quite uncertain.[25] There is no indication whether the *legis actio per iudicis postulationem* is older than the Twelve Tables, but that code provided it as the action on the *stipulatio* and for the division of an inheritance.[26] At least from that date, the statement *testes estote* would be inappropriate for this *legis actio* since the code specifically used the terms *iudex* 'judge' and *arbiter*. Nor could *testes estote* appear in the *legis actio per condictionem*—which is later than the Twelve Tables, introduced by the *lex Silia* and the *lex Calpurnia*— because the judge also was appointed only thirty days after the proceedings *in iure*. So far as we have evidence then, the wording *testes estote* would be quite obsolete in *legis actiones* from the date of the *lex Pinaria,* whenever that was; and, moreover, the word *iudex* was a term used to signify the judge from the time of the Twelve Tables. This is helpful in understanding the verbal history.

It is instructive to plot the most plausible history of the words *testis* and *iudex* in this context. We may proceed from three fixed, or relatively fixed, points.

1. *Testis* was the old word used in treaties and declarations of war to signify 'judge'. Livy's account places this use of the term as early as the regal period. Likewise in the most archaic *legis actio,* that *sacramento, testis* signified 'judge'. Even if the *legis actio sacramento* does not reach back to the regal period, it is earlier than the Twelve Tables.

2. The term iudex was used in the early Republic to designate the chief official of the state, who was later called consul. The evidence, though sparse, is plain and widely accepted.[27] Indeed, Dumézil suggests that the *rex* was first replaced in his political functions by a *iudex* or *praetor*.[28] For our purposes, the most important text is Varro, *De lingua latina,* 6.88:

> In the *Consular Commentaries* I found the following: "Let he who is about to summon the army say to his assistant, 'Gaius Calpurnius, call all the citizens here to me.' The assistant declares, 'All citizens, come you here to the *iudices*.' The consul says, 'Gaius Calpurnius, call all the citizens to me, to a gathering.' The assistant declares, 'All citizens, come

to the gathering, here to the iudices.' Then the consul declares to the army, 'I order you to go the proper way to the *comitia centuriata*.' "[29]

The meaning 'judge' for *iudex* clearly is excluded here. The importance of this text over the others is that *iudex* is used here of the magistrate in a military context. There is thus no foundation for the view, sometimes expressed,[30] that in the early Republic *iudex* is the supreme magistrate in his civil capacity, *praetor* is the same magistrate in his military guise.[31] Hence, when used in this way, *iudex* does not have a secondary sense of 'judge'. This confirms that *iudex* derives from *ius dicere* 'to declare the law', not from *iudicare* 'to judge'.[32] Semantically, it corresponds indeed to the Oscan *meddix,* which Festus tells us was an Oscan term for a magistrate.[33] Thus, there would be no support for a proposition that *iudex* in Latin originally meant 'judge'.

It is also most unlikely that *iudex* was ever a title of the Roman kings. A supreme ruler has no need for a title designating one or more of his functions. Moreover, the texts are unanimous that this is a title applied to the consul.

The term *consul* is relatively late, the word *praetor* previously expressing the supreme magistrate.[34]

From this early history of *iudex,* we can produce another argument for the early meaning of *testis. Iudex* originally did not mean 'judge'. But some term must surely have existed to designate the judge. What other possibility can there be but *testis?*

3. *Iudex* was used to mean 'judge' as early as the Twelve Tables.[35]

From these fixed points we can, I believe, postulate the following verbal development. In very early Rome *testis* 'third party' was the usual term for judge. The word *iudex* existed and designated the chief magistrates. In that context it was superseded by the term *praetor.* Instead of disappearing, *iudex* took on the meaning of 'judge'. *Testis* was not free from ambiguity, perhaps particularly because in declarations of war others as well as gods were called upon to hear, though not to judge. The word *testis* was, I suggest, naturally extended in thought to include the *pater patratus,* boundaries, and *fas,* who were not judges, but whose function was to

17

witness. In time as *iudex* became the standard term for judge, *testis* became restricted in meaning to 'witness'.

No argument can be drawn against the foregoing from the wording of the old form of will which made use of the ceremony of *mancipatio,* the formal mode of transferring the important types of property known as *res mancipi.* The making of the will was in two stages. In the first stage, the person who was to act as the recipient of the testator's property, declared in the presence of five adult Roman citizens who acted as witnesses: "I declare that your family and property are subject to your wishes and in my custody, and let them have been bought by me with this copper and these scales so that you can make a will in accordance with the public statute."[36] He then struck the scales he was holding with a piece of bronze, which he gave to the testator as if it were the price. This is the wording given by Gaius in his *Institutes,* 2.104. That originally, in my view, the formulation did not contain the word *familiam* need not detain us.[37] What matters is that *secundum legem publicam* 'in accordance with the public statute' refers to the Twelve Tables. The Twelve Tables did not aim at a complete statement of the law, and there was a particular reason for each clause. In this instance the codification in the appropriate clause (*Tab.* 5.3), gave legal recognition to a preexisting practice. Romans had in fact been in the practice of making testamentary dispositions in this way, and the code now gave the ceremony legal effect. The wording comes in part at least from the time after that codification. But we are mainly concerned with the *nuncupatio,* the declaration made by the testator: "These things as they have been written on these tablets and wax, so I give, so I bequeath, so I call to witness, and so do you, citizens, bear me witness."[38] In this, the words *testor* and *testimonium* must mean 'I call to witness' and 'the act of bearing witness', respectively. There is no reference here to judging. But the *nuncupatio* will be later than the first part of the ceremony, the declaration by the *familiae emptor,* which alone corresponds to the *mancipatio,* and which in some ways is later than the Twelve Tables. Indeed, there was no need for the *nuncupatio,* and it need not have occurred at all, especially when the "will" was written. Above all, even if *testor* and *testimonium* in the *nuncupatio* predate the Twelve

Tables, that would be no argument that then the word *testis* could not also refer to judging. There will have been a time when the meanings of the word overlapped. Indeed, nothing excludes the possibility that even at the outset the word contained the meaning of witnessing as well as of judging.[39]

At the risk of appearing to use a circular argument I would urge that the fact that *testes* meaning judges makes *litis contestatio* more understandable is further confirmation that in Roman declarations of war the gods, as *testes,* are judges.

Significantly for what comes later in this book, Dieter Nörr, who takes *testis* to mean 'witness', says: "One can attempt to dispute the legal character of the Roman interational law only if one were to make a non-partisan decision maker an essential feature of a legal regime."[40] I take Nörr to mean that for him there was no nonpartisan decisionmaker (or judge) in Roman declarations of war and that, in other respects, Roman international law had all the necessary characteristics of law, hence it ought to be classified as law unless one insisted that a judge was a necessary feature of a legal system. I would make a nonpartisan decision maker an essential feature of a legal regime, and I do find such a figure in Roman international law.[41]

# Three

# Declarations of War

As was stressed in the previous chapter, the fetials' declarations of war have the form of a *legis actio* of private law; but that does not mean they have the form of any one particular *legis actio*. Just as the *legis actio sacramento* differs in form from the *legis actio per iudicis postulationem,* and both differ again from the *legis actio per condictionem,* so declarations of war differ in form from all three of these *legis actiones.* They also differ in form from treaties. That the parallel of declarations of war is with actions at private law, not with criminal trials, is entirely appropriate. In the first place, the primary Roman actions for such wrongs as theft (*furtum*), wrongful damage to property (*damnum iniuria datum*), physical assault and insult (*iniuria*), and subsequently robbery with violence (*rapina*) were all at private law. Second, it would be inconsistent with the dignity of the approach to regard the enemy as a criminal; rather, the opponent is treated as being on the same level.

The point that must be made here is not that declarations of war derive in form from *legis actiones* (or even vice versa). There is no indication of any such indebtedness. Rather, they are parallel developments. The Roman declaration of war takes a legal form because the Romans were so legalistic. Roman religion partakes of this legalism, which is found in the art and science of both the *pontifices* and the *augures*. Now we also find it among the *fetiales*.

The best source of our information is from Livy both for treaties and for declarations of war. Only for the former do we have information on the proceedings at Rome, before the fetial set out for foreign territory, and these were looked at in chapter 1.[1] The declarations (called *clarigatio*)[2] in front of the enemy took place in three stages.

> 1.32.6. When the envoy reaches the boundaries of the people from whom restitution is sought, he covers his head with a cap, the covering is of wool, and he says, "Hear Jupiter; hear you boundaries"—he names of which people—"Let righteousness hear. I am the public messenger of the Roman people. Duly and righteously commissioned, I come. Let faith be given to my words." He recites his demands. 7. Then he makes Jupiter judge [*testis*]: "If I wrongfully and contrary to religion demand that those men and those things be surrendered to me, then let me never enjoy my native land."[3]

The recitation of demands in section 6 means that the legal claim was akin to that of the *legis actio per condictionem:* "I declare it is proper that you give me ten thousand *sestertii.*"[4] The *condictio* was an action in which the plaintiff claimed that the defendant was under an obligation to deliver something to him, something, however, of which the plaintiff was not owner. From sections 7 and 9 we learn that the fetial's demand is for the surrender of men and property. If the men in question are members of the Aequicoli tribe—they are the enemy in this instance—then this comparison with a *condictio* is appropriate, since they are not owned by the Roman people or the fetial; likewise, if they were Roman citizens who had been captured, since by capture they would have ceased to be Romans and have become slaves of the enemy.[5] Again, Roman citizens lost ownership of any property taken by the enemy.[6] Although the demands in section 6 are similar to the structure of the *legis actio per condictionem,* we should note that the *condictio* postdates the fetial's formulation.

Section 7 contains a declaration akin to an oath, with a penalty to be imposed on the fetial in the event of a breach.[7] This is reminiscent of the procedure in the old *legis actio sacramento*. In the form of that called *in rem,* both parties made a claim of ownership, an oath was taken in the sum of fifty or five hundred *asses* according to the value of the disputed object, the trial then proceeded on the veracity of the oath, and the losing party forfeited the amount of the oath.[8]

The fetial formally establishes that he is acting as a representative: "I am the public messenger of the Roman people. Duly and righteously commissioned I come." Though in contrast to the later formulary procedure, representation in the *legis actiones* was restricted to very particular cases, these cases are in fact relevant here:

> G.4.82. We must next observe that we may bring an action in our own name or in that of another, as his *cognitor, procurator, tutor,* or *curator,* though formerly, at the time when the *legis actiones* were in use, it was not permitted to act on behalf of another, except in certain cases.[9]

*J.4.10pr.* expands on these special cases:

> We must now point out that one may take proceedings in one's own name or in that of another. In the name of another, as a procurator, tutor, or curator; for, at one time, there could be no action on behalf of another save on behalf of the people, in respect of liberty or as a guardian. Further, it was provided by the *lex Hostilia* that a theft action might be brought in the name of those who are in enemy hands or absent on public service or for those who are in their guardianship. And, because there was no small inconvenience in the fact that it was not permissible either to sue or defend an action in the name of another, men began to litigate through procurators: for sickness, age, the need to go abroad, and many other occasions are often an obstacle to persons pressing their claims in person.[10]

It is often suggested that the actions brought *pro populo* 'on behalf of the people', are the *actiones populares,* that is actions that could be brought by anyone,[11] but as Thomas observes, these are scarcely cases of representation.[12] More to the point, as Kaser stresses, these *actiones populares* are all actions created by the praetor and hence must be later.[13] He himself thinks rather of a private citizens or magistrate claiming on behalf of the state a piece of land from a private individual.[14] However, this may be, it is sufficient for present purposes to notice that in the *legis actio* process, a representative could act for another in certain circumstances, primarily where a party was unable to act for himself; that, according to G.4.73, the *cognitor* was appointed with formal words; and the fetial claims to have been duly and righteously appointed to act for the Roman people. A people, of course, could only act through a representative.

The significance of all this for us is precisely that any condemnation arising from the private law action would lie for or against the representative, the *cognitor,* and not his principal:

> G.4.86. A man suing on account of another frames the *intentio* in the name of his principal, but transfers the *condemnatio* into his own name.[15]

In this instance, the fetial likewise demands on behalf of the people but turns the result of a wrongful claim against himself, and not against the Roman people: "If I wrongfully and contrary to religion demand that those men and those things be surrendered to me, then let me never enjoy my native land." The parallel with private law is extreme. The fetial pronounces this formulation with a few changes when he enters the enemy's boundaries, to the first man he meets, when he enters the city gates, again when he enters the forum.[16]

We learn from section 5 that the Roman fetial involved is the *pater patratus* and that he makes demands from the other, in this instance Alban, *pater patratus.* Presumably this is the declaration made just inside the enemy boundaries or in the forum where, according to Dionysius of Halicarnassus, 2.72.7, he discussed with the magistrates the reasons for his coming. The fetial's task is not so risky as it may appear since by the law of all nations the person of a priest and legate was held to be inviolable.[17] But there is in this mutuality another parallelism with a Roman *legis actio.* We may presume that the *pater patratus* of each side called upon the same god or gods to judge—the Latin peoples, including the Romans had certain religious rites in common. So the *patres patrati* were choosing the judge. Likewise, as was observed in the preceding chapter, in private law actions the two opposing parties selected the judge.

If the demands are not met, there is a pause of thirty-three days according to Livy, 1.32.9; then the fetial declares war. Livy, 1.22.5, gives the pause as thirty days, and Dionysius of Halicarnassus says that, if the other side needed time to deliberate, the fetial gave them ten days, then repeated the formula, and did the same again after another ten days. This pause of thirty or thirty-three days corresponds in some respects, but not in others, to the pause of thirty days to choose a judge in the formal *legis actio per condictionem*: "Since you deny, I give you notice [*condico*] to appear in thirty days in order to take a judge."[18] After the *lex Pinaria* a similar delay in choosing the judge occurred in the *legis actio sacramento*. But in the declaration of war, the judge, Jupiter, as in the early *legis actio sacramento,* has already been chosen. The nature of the difference in function of the thirty days' pause best emerges a little later in this chapter.

After this pause, the fetial makes the following claim:

> Livy, 1.32.9. "Hear, Jupiter, and you Janus Quirinus, and hear all heavenly gods, and you, gods of earth, and you of the lower world; 10. I call you to judge that this people"—naming whatever people it is—"is unjust, and does not make just reparation. But of these matters we will take counsel of the elders in our country, how we may obtain our right."[19]

Some of the issues raised by this complex declaration are best left until later in the chapter. As will be seen, it represents a second legal procedure. At the present moment our concern is only with the final part of the declaration: "But of these matters we will take counsel of the elders in our country, how we may obtain our right."

The words indicate that a judgment has already been given and, at that, in favor of the Romans. Some elaboration is required. The recitation of the fetial recorded by Livy in 1.32.6–7 corresponds to the first and formal stage of a *legis actio,* that termed *in iure* and which was held before a state official, and ended (in the *legis actio sacramento*) by the appointment of a judge. The second stage, that *apud iudicem,* in which the judge heard the case and gave his decision, was presumably less formal, but we have no discussion of it by the jurists. The equivalent for declarations of war of this second stage is also passed over, but it has occurred before the fetial's recitation in Livy, 1.32.9–10.

It will be remembered that in Roman private law, the state provided no machinery for the execution of a judgment. Likewise here, after the gods have given a judgment in favor of the Romans, the Romans themselves have to enforce their adjudged right. This interpretation is confirmed by the next steps recorded by Livy.

> 1.32.10. . . . Then the messenger returns to Rome for consultation. Immediately the king would consult the senators in almost these words: 11. "Regarding those things, lawsuits, those causes, concerning which the *pater patratus* of the Roman people made demands [*condixit*] on the *pater patratus* of the Ancient Latins, and on the men of the Ancient Latins, which things they did not surrender, nor pay, nor fulfill, being things which it was proper [*oportuit*] to surrender, pay, fulfill, speak," he said to him whose opinion he first asked, "What do you think?" 12. Then the other replied: "I think that these things ought to be sought in a pure and righteous war, and so I consent and vote." Then, in order, the others were asked; and when a majority of those present went over to the same opinion, war had been agreed upon.[20]

The terms *res, lites,* and *causae* are typical of legal Latin.[21] The verb *condicere* 'to make demands' is also a legal term, as in the *legis actio per condictionem*. Again, in legal Latin, the verb *oportet* means 'it is proper according to higher authority'.[22] Hence, *oportuit* in the perfect tense means that the claim was held proper by the higher authority, namely in this instance Jupiter. The decision to fight a war is only a decision on how to enforce the judgment of Jupiter.

Livy continues:

> 1.32.12. . . . The practice was that the fetial would carry a cornel-wood spear[23] with an iron[24] or fire-hardened point to their boundaries, and, in the presence of no fewer than three persons over puberty would say: 13. "Whereas the peoples of the Ancient Latins and the men of the Ancient Latins have acted, and been guilty of wrongs, against the Roman people of the Quirites, whereas the Roman people of the Quirites commanded that there be war with the Ancient Latins, and

the senate of the Roman people of the Quirites approved, agreed and voted that war should be made with the Ancient Latins; I therefore, and the Roman people, declare and make war with the peoples of the Ancient Latins and the men of the Ancient Latins." When he had said that he would hurl his spear into their territory. 14. This is the way that at that time redress was sought from the Latins and war declared: and later generations accepted the custom.[25]

As I stated before, there was no direct state enforcement of a private law judgment. But if a judgment debtor did not perform, then there could be another *legis actio* of a very different type, namely *legis actio per manus iniectionem,* the *legis actio* by laying on of hands. If the judgment debt remained unsatisfied for thirty days after the judgment, the creditor could bring his opponent before the magistrate. Gaius describes the procedure:

> G.4.21. Likewise one proceeded by *manus iniectio* for those matters in which by some statute it was laid down so to proceed, for instance for a judgment debt under the Twelve Tables. The action was as follows: the plaintiff said: "Whereas you are indebted to me by judgment (or 'by condemnation') in ten thousand sesterces, and whereas you have not paid, on that account I lay my hand on you for ten thousand sesterces of judgment debt"; and at the same time he laid hold of some part of the debtor's body. It was not permitted for the debtor to throw off the hand himself, and to conduct the *legis actio* for himself, but he gave a *vindex* [guarantor] who conducted it for him. Whoever did not give a *vindex* was led off home by the plaintiff and put in chains.[26]

This parallels the last act of the fetial's declaration. For both, the delay of thirty days was to allow the adjudged opponent time to make proper performance. The seizing by the hand of the person of the debtor for the judgment debt is matched by the throwing of the spear into the enemy's territory both following upon, in the one case, the claim of a judgment debt, in the other the claim that the enemy had been found guilty (by the god) of wrongs. One cannot, of course, follow the parallelism in every detail. *Manus iniectio* could occur only when the debt was established to be a fixed sum of money. In war, the debt could not be so established in advance. Restraints were imposed upon the person of the judgment debtor after *manus iniectio*. We can only conjecture whether the enemy was supposed to suffer analogous constraints after this third stage. The extent of the parallel with private law is, of course, remarkable.

We are now in a position to return to the middle declaration of the fetial to the enemy. The first declaration corresponds to the formally worded part of the *legis actio* in front of the magistrate, *in iure*. The third corresponds to the *legis actio per manus iniectionem,* which, in the absence of direct state enforcement of a judgment, ensued when the judgment debtor did not pay up after the allotted time.

The second declaration of the fetial, however, does not correspond to the second stage of a "*legis actio* in front of the judge, *apud iudicem,* which, although we have no evidence, we can assume did not involve formal words.[27] Nor could this second declaration have any such function. At that stage, witnesses give evidence, and the judge gives the judgment. That stage, where Jupiter who has been appointed Judge gives judgment, cannot be represented. Instead, the second declaration is a second set of proceedings *in iure*. But they are proceedings *in iure* with a difference. The gods are to judge not that the Albans ought properly to give something to the Romans, but that the Albans are unjust and fail to make reparation. That is to say, the second declaration proceeds on the assumption that Jupiter has already given judgment after the first call to act as judge. He has found the Albans at fault; but, still, they have not made restitution. That the Albans have failed to make restitution though they have been found at fault is what the gods are now asked to find as judges. This explains why, although only Jupiter is to be judge in the first declaration, all the gods are called upon to be judges in the second. This second proceeding *in iure* has for the Romans a very practical purpose. It puts on record that Jupiter gave his verdict for the Romans.

This approach to the declaration of war has important consequences. First, the Romans have the psychological advantage of knowing, even before the fighting begins, that they have the verdict of the gods. Their war is just. Second, this conclusion is not shaken even by a Roman defeat. A defeat in the just war shows that the Romans were unable to execute the gods' judgment. Execution of judgment is not the affair of the gods. Third, a breach of faith after a treaty or declaration of war has, as its secular equivalent, contempt of court. It is notorious that as a general rule judges treat contempt of court as an offense of great seriousness. Breach of faith brings down the wrath of the gods.

Very significantly, and from our perspective appropriately, the Roman declaration of war makes no demand upon Mars, the god of war, to be *testis*.[28] The god of war is not a proper person to be judge in a lawsuit.[29] Again, during the course of the war, the Romans made prayers to the gods, asking them to be propitious, and they make vows to the gods, promising them something in return for favors, but this present behavior should not be seen as asking favors from or offering bribes to judges. The gods have already fulfilled their role of judging.

This approach to declarations of war also means that the Romans' had two requirements for a *iustum bellum*. The first, as we have already seen in a number of texts, is a formal declaration made in the proper way.[30] But we have further testimony:

> Nonius, 529. Fetials among the Old Romans were those who, in the holy office of ambassadors, demanded in legal form, making a treaty, the pledges from those who had served with hostile intent against the Roman people by force or rapine or assault. Nor were wars declared, those at least termed pious, before there was a declaration from the fetials.
>
> Varro writes in "On the Life of the Roman People": "And thus wars were declared both late and with great care because they thought no war ought to be waged unless it was pious. And before they declared war, they sent to the people whom they knew to have committed wrongs four fetials whom they called orators, as ambassadors to seek restitution."[31]

Other texts, especially from Cicero, are to the same effect.[32]

But the very form of the declaration entailed a second requirement. There had to be a just cause of war, and the other people must have refused to make redress. The *patter patratus* insists: "If I wrongfully and contrary to religion demand that those men and those things be surrendered to me, then let me never enjoy my native land."[33] A just cause might be failure to return men or property that had been seized, to offer redress for a violated ambassador, or to repulse an enemy attack. The care that was needed to ensure both that the proper procedure was scrupulously observed and that the cause was just emerges from a passage of Livy for the year 427 B.C.:

> 4.30.12. Revenge on the people of Veii was postponed until the following year, when Gaius Servillius Ahala and Lucius Papirius Mugillanus were consuls, 13. Even then religious observance was an obstacle to war being declared at once and the armies being sent into the field: they decided that fetials had first to be sent to demand restitution. 14. Not long before there had been a battle with the Veientes near Nomentum and Fidenae, and then a truce had been made but not peace. Even the time of that had run out and the enemy had begun to fight before that day. Still fetials were sent, but their words were not listened to when they sought restitution, and had sworn according to ancient custom. 15. A dispute then arose whether war would be declared by the command of the people or whether a decree of the senate was sufficient. The tribunes prevailed by threatening to hinder the levy, forcing the consul Quinctius to carry the question of war to the people. 16. All of the centuries voted for it. In this, too, the plebs had the better of it, that they obtained that consuls would not be elected for the following year.[34]

The care taken to observe the correct procedure is particularly noteworthy since Veii was an Etruscan city and not known to have *fetiales*.

The text brings out another point that also has appeared in other texts. The decision of the fetials was that a just war could be waged, but they could not determine that a war should be waged. That was a decision in the earliest days of the king and senate and then, with the growth in power of the plebeians, of the people.[35] The point at issue in the dispute at the end of Levy's account is whether this is a new war, or the continuation of the previous one. If it was a new war the consent of the people was needed, but not otherwise.

No individual, not even the most senior, could wage a just war without the consent of the people.[36]

The fetial system was devised to keep the peace or, if all else failed, ensure that the gods declared a legal verdict in favor of the Romans before fighting began. The formulation required the Romans have a just cause for the war. But the system in its pure form required mutuality, the other side also having fetials.[37] Accordingly, in one sense from an early date it was increasingly in trouble. Fetials eventually ceased to be used in declarations of war and secular ambassadors were used instead. This matter will be discussed subsequently. What concerns us now is the issue whether the Romans still required in theory a just cause for a just war, once the declaration was made by secular authorities. We are remarkably ill-informed. Our information comes from two passages of Cicero which have survived from Isidorus. They may seem to conflict:

> *De re publica,* 3.23.35. Those wars are unjust that are undertaken without cause. For there can be no just war without a cause in vengeance or to repulse an enemy.[38]

According to this a just cause was needed. But we also have the evidence of what appears to be a continuation of the same text:

> No war is considered to be just unless it has been proclaimed or declared or unless reparation has been demanded.[39]

On its face this tells us that a war is just if the formalities have been observed.[40] What we cannot discover is the original relationship between the two passages. If they were originally together, then Cicero would be saying that a just cause was needed for a proper war. But we still would not know whether this was the official, orthodox, "state" position, or whether, as often, Cicero was simply being moralistic.

I said that in one sense the fetial system was increasingly in trouble from an early date because in its pure form the ceremonial required that the other side also have fetials; and states other than some Latin or related peoples had none. And so it was, and fetials came to be generally replaced by law ambassadors. But in another sense, so long as the system operated, the absence of fetials from the other warring state, such as an Etruscan city, increased the Roman psychological advantage. Only the Romans had the verdict of the gods that their war was just.

# Four

# Treaty Making

n contrast to declarations of war, Roman treaties have no close
analogue in private law even though in part they are, in effect,
contracts, though of an international kind.

Here, too, we are indebted to Livy for the formulation. After
a fetial was created *pater patratus,* he was appointed Rome's
official envoy or spokesman by the king in order, says Livy, "to
bring the oath to completion, that is, to solemnize the treaty. He
accomplishes this with many words, expressed in a long metrical
formula, which is not worthwhile to quote."[1]

Livy continues:

> 1.24.7. When the terms have been recited, he says: "Hear, Jupiter,
> hear, *pater patratus* of the Alban people; hear, you, Alban people. As
> these terms from first to last have been publicly recited from these
> tablets or wax, without fraud and as they are today most correctly
> understood, from these terms the Roman people will not be the first
> to defect."[2]

To this point, the treaty has the form of a contract, an oral contract
at that, but it is quite unlike any contract of Roman private law,
including the *stipulatio,* which was the most important oral contract. To begin with, Jupiter, the Alban *pater patratus,* and the

31

Alban people are called on to be witnesses. There is no legal role for witnesses in the formulation of Roman contracts, and certainly not in the oral *stipulatio*. Witnesses were needed, though, for the ceremony of *mancipatio,* which was used to transfer certain important kinds of property, for its derivatives such as adoption, and for the so-called praetorian will. But for the treaty, the purpose of witnessing is different. Although called as witnesses they are not to keep note in order to provide evidence if a dispute subsequently arises as to meaning. Rather, apart from Jupiter who is actually to act as judge, they are interested parties—indeed, the parties to the contract. They have to know what the Romans are promising them. A second difference is that in the *stipulatio* it is the person to whom the promise is being made who sets out the terms of the contract: in the treaty it is the promisor. Third, there is no reciprocal exchange of words in this formulation of the treaty as there is in a *stipulatio.*[3] Although there was presumably a similar formulation by the Alban *pater patratus,*[4] the two declarations are not technically linked."[5] But on the other hand the declarations are exactly what one finds in the legalese of other Roman religious formulations. Notable examples, especially with regard to the cautelary phrases, occur in the vows of the priests of the Arval brothers. For instance, in a vow made on January 3, A.D. 81, to Jupiter for the safety of Titus and Domitian, the rulers are qualified as "those whom we intend to name," and the petitioners request a happy outcome "as we intend to state the same."[6] Livy himself, recording a vow, has a declaration made at 22.10.2, "If the state of the Roman people shall be preserved for the next five years—as I would wish it to be preserved."

The precautionary phrase "as they are today most correctly understood" is, so far as I am aware, unparalleled in private law. Indeed, the words are inappropriate for a dispute that would subsequently arise before a human judge, since he is not really usually in a position to know how the terms were correctly understood when they were recited.

It is in this cautelary context that I would, following Dumézil, place the formulation of the treaty, *ex illis tabulis cerave recitata* ("recited from these tablets or wax").[7] There are more possibilities than one,[8] but his preferred hypothesis (and mine) is that *tabulis cerave* form part of a unitary text and refer to wooden tablets coated with wax for writing. According to this view *cerave* is a precaution against a trick of interpretation by mental reservation: "These clauses as they have been read from these tablets or, if you prefer, from the wax that is on them."[9]

Livy's discussion of the formulation of the treaty goes on:

> 8. "If it [the Roman people] should by public consent and fraudulently first depart from them, then, do you, Jupiter, so strike the Roman people as I strike this pig this day; strike so much the more as your power and strength are greater." 9. When he said this he struck the pig with a flint knife. Likewise the Albans performed their formulation and their oath through their dictator and their priests.[10]

This is the part of the ceremony which presumably contains the oath mentioned at section 6. After the call in section 7, to Jupiter, the Alban *pater patratus,* and the Alban people, to witness, only Jupiter is called upon to smite the Roman people. From a modern perspective, it is the Albans who should take action against the Romans. Moreover, so far as a treaty is a contract, they are the other contracting party. But that role of avenger is reserved for Jupiter because of the declaration to him. Breach of a treaty properly and formally made with the Albans is a breach of faith with Jupiter. For this he is to exact punishment. It should be noted, however, that this does not make Jupiter a judge. There is no trial.

Reuven Yaron, who is primarily concerned with Carthaginian treaties, observes correctly that the gods do not simply play the passive role of witnesses.[11] And he declares they are guarantors of the treaties. I find no indication in the sources that the gods were regarded as guarantors.[12]

In contrast to the form of a declaration of war given by Livy in 1.24, a breach of the treaty is to be followed by punishment of the people. Likewise at 9.5.3, Livy says that a treaty is concluded by a prayer "that the people responsible for any departure from the stated terms be struck by Jupiter, just as the pig is struck by the fetials." The sacrifice of a pig struck by a stone was so associated with treaty making that the grammarian Servius could give *foede* 'horribly, disgustingly' as an alternative etymology for the word *foedus* 'treaty': "or from a pig killed *foede,* that is, by stones."[13]

The vow here, if that term is really appropriate, is very different from that typically found. The typical form is: "If you [the deity] do [give victory], I will do [dedicate a temple]." This vow in making a treaty inverts the relationship: "If the Romans do [break the treaty], then do you, deity [smite]." In the typical vow the Roman promises to do something for the deity, if the deity first gives the required result. In this, the Roman acts first (breaking the treaty) and then the deity is to perform.

The fetial system in a pure form would begin to break down as soon as Rome extended its sphere of interest from central Italy, for only there did other peoples have fetials. This must have occurred early. According to Polybius, the first treaty with Carthage was made in the first year of the Republic.[14]

But such is the power of tradition that the system continued. The role of the fetials in treaty making survived longer than their role in declaring war. A particularly striking example comes from 201 B.C. when a peace treaty was to be made in Africa with the Carthaginians:

> Livy, 30.43.9. When the fetials were ordered to go to Africa to strike a treaty, a decree of the senate was passed at their own request in these words, that they should each take a stone of flint and the herb so that when the Roman praetor ordered them to strike the treaty, they could demand from him the sacred herb. It is customary for that type of plant taken from the citadel to be given to the fetials."[15]

The force of tradition is such that the Roman ceremony to be performed in Africa mirrors that in Rome, except, of course, that the Carthaginians have no fetials with whom the Romans can interact. We can properly assume, however, that the fetials would only so be used on particularly solemn occasions.

Carefully to be distinguished from a treaty (*foedus*), especially in early times, was the guarantee (*sponsio*) of a general.[16] The most notable example relates to the agreement made in 321 B.C. after the Samnites trapped the Roman army in the Caudine Forks, and no escape was possible:

Livy, 9.5.1. The consuls went to confer with Pontius [the Sabine leader]. The victor proposed a treaty, but they denied that a treaty could be made without the command of the people, and without the fetials and the rest of the solemn ceremonial. 2. Thus, the Caudine peace was not, as is commonly believed, entered into by a treaty, but was made by a guarantee. 3. For what need was there for guarantors or hostages in a treaty where the agreement is concluded with a prayer, that the people responsible for departing from the recited clauses would be struck by Jupiter, just as the pig is struck by the fetial?[17]

Thus, there was no treaty but a *sponsio,* a guarantee, given by the consuls and other leading men, and there were hostages.[18] Accordingly, there was no treaty, with religious obligations, and the Romans did not regard it as a breach of faith, punishable by the gods, to go back on it. Subsequently, the (now former) consul, Spurius Postumius, who had guaranteed the agreement, addressed the newly elected consuls:

Livy, 9.8.4. . . . My proposal will bear witness whether I spared myself or your legions when I bound myself to a vile or necessary guarantee: 5. by which, since it was made without the authorization of the Roman people, the Roman people is not bound. Nothing is owed under it to the Samnites but our own bodies. 6. Let us, naked and bound, be surrendered by the fetials. Let us release the people from their religious obligation, if we have bound them in any way, so that there is no obstacle, divine or human, to entering again upon a just and pious war.[19]

Postumius argues that even if the guarantee put the Roman people under an obligation to the gods, still, there was no treaty by the people, the surrender of the guarantors would satisfy any obligation to the gods and men. There was no need, he claimed, to surrender the whole army that had been in the grip of the Samnites.

Livy, 9.10.8. Then on arriving at the assembly of the Samnites and the tribunal of Pontius, Aulus Cornelius Arvina, the fetial, spoke words as follows: "Whereas these men, without authorization from the Roman people of the Quirites guaranteed that a treaty would be struck and on that account they committed a wrong; on that account so that the Roman people should be released from an impious crime, I surrender these men to you."[20]

Ziegler believes that clearly the *sponsio* of the Roman official, strengthened by an oath, bound the Roman people just as would a *foedus* struck by the fetials.[21] This proposition is not warranted for the middle Republic, as shown by these passages from Livy. The whole point of Livy's treatment is that the Romans were not bound by the general's *sponsio* to perform its terms. (It may be recalled that no one can bind another person to performance in the *sponsio* or *stipulatio* of private law.) There are various legal strands in the Livy passages, and they must be disentangled.

First, in Livy, 9.8.4, Spurius Postumus claims that he bound himself by the *sponsio,* but (in 9.8.5) that he did not bind the Roman people because he acted without its authorization. Nothing is owed to the Samnites—he does not say by whom—except, he says, the bodies of himself and his colleagues. Why precisely this act of surrender should be the result of the oath is not immediately plain. The position does not correspond to Roman private contract law. The position there until the late second century A.D. was that one could not promise the act of another, and such a *stipulatio* was void.[22]

Second, in Livy, 9.8.6, Postumius concedes that possibly his *sponsio* did bind the Roman people in a religious way, but that obligation, if it existed, would be ended by the surrender of the defaulting individuals.

Third, as we have seen, according to Livy, 9.10.9, when the fetial surrendered the guarantors of peace with the Samnites, he declared: "Whereas these men, without authorization from the Roman people of the Quirites guaranteed that a treaty would be struck and on that account they committed a wrong [*noxam nocuerunt*]; on that account so that the Roman people should be released from an impious crime, I surrender these men to you." The expression *noxam nocere* or *noxiam nocere* 'to commit a wrong' is standard in legal Latin, even if it may not be quite technical. Indeed, it appears in the archaic code of the Twelve Tables (at *Tab.* 12.2a): "Si servus furtum faxit noxiamve noxit" ("If a slave commits theft or commits a wrong"). Although we do not have the wording of the rest of the clause, the import of the provision was that when a slave committed a wrong and the owner was not directly involved in the wrongdoing, the owner could free himself from all other liability by surrendering the slave to the victim.[23] And when the phrase *noxiam nocere* appears in the Roman legal sources, it is always used of a slave committing a wrong.[24] Not only slaves but also sons in power (*in potestate*) could be so noxally surrendered in classical and earlier law,[25] and a similar procedure was also available for wrongdoing animals. Accordingly, Livy's account of the *deditio* of individuals is peculiarly appropriate: just as a Roman could surrender to the victim a person in power who had committed a wrong (*noxam nocere*) without his authorization, and so release himself from all further liability, so the Roman state could surrender to the injured people citizens subject to its power who had committed wrongs without authorization, and so release itself from all further liability. This precision goes beyond Livy's use of language. There is a direct correspondence between the private law institution of noxal surrender and the *deditio* of an individual.

It is this third strand that is most illuminating, and not just for its connection with private law. Livy here, I suggest, is giving us the gist not only of this declaration, but of all declarations made when the fetials of any people surrendered one of their citizens. The opposing fetials had demanded the surrender of an individual; failure to surrender would result in war. The people to whom the demand is made is treated as being under an obligation. But that obligation can be totally extinguished by surrendering the wrongdoer. This is independent of the nature of the wrong that was committed. That is to say that in the present context the surrender was offered not because of a Roman obligation specifically arising from the general's *sponsio,* but simply because of a wrong committed by the general against the Samnites.

# Five

# Cautelary Jurisprudence
# and Judgments

s we have seen, an important part of the fetials'
duties was to make the formal demand of a foreign
people for restitution of wrongs, such as the surrender of persons who had offended against Rome.[1]
Likewise they had the function of determining
whether Rome or a Roman had offended against a foreign state
and what should be done. Their jurisdiction was even wider and
extended to all questions of what ought properly and religiously
to be done with regard to declarations of war. A prime example
for the year 191 B.C. appears in Livy.

> 36.3.7. Then the consul Manius Acilius, following the decree of the
> senate laid the question before the college of fetials whether the declara-
> tion of war should be made to King Antiochus himself, or whether it
> was enough that it be announced at some garrison of his; 8. and
> whether also they ordered the war to be formally proclaimed separately
> to the Aetolians and whether the alliance and friendship with them
> had to be renounced before war was declared. 9. The fetials replied
> that they had already decided, when they were consulted about Philip,
> that it made no difference whether the declaration was made to him
> personally or at a garrison. 10. Friendship seemed to have been already
> renounced, they claimed, because they had voted that after ambassa-

dors had so often demanded it, restitution had not been made nor fair satisfaction given. 11. Further, the Aetolians had already declared war on them, when they had occupied by force Demetrias, a city of their allies, 12. had proceeded to besiege Chalcis by land and sea, and had brought king Antiochus to Europe to wage war on the Roman people.[2]

When so consulted, the fetials acted as a college and not through representatives.[3] The passage shows how law and religion were intertwined. The question put was a legal one, so was the answer, and, on the face of it, the subject matter was also legal, but the persons responsible for the answer were priests. That the question was put at all to the fetials shows that part of their functions was changing with the growing empire of Rome. In the early days of Rome's history, it was the fetials themselves who would have made the claims for restitution, and the *pater patratus* would have uttered the declaration of war. But with the expansion of Rome's field of operations beyond central Italy, opposing peoples had no fetials and no *pater patratus*. The previous occasion, when the consul consulted the fetials about war with King Philip, occurred in 200 B.C.[4]

From 188 B.C. we have an example of Roman citizens being surrendered to an enemy, the Carthaginians, for striking ambassadors:[5]

> Valerius Maximus, 6.6.3. The senators showed similar faith toward the same enemies in protecting the law of embassies. For when Aemilius Lepidus and Lucius Flaminius were consuls they saw to it through the praetor Marcus Claudius that Lucius Minucius and Lucius Manlius were surrendered by the fetials to the ambassadors of the Carthaginians, because they had assaulted them. At that time the senate had regard for itself, not for those to whom this performance was made.[6]

The wording of the last sentence indicates that on this occasion, the senate itself decided on the surrender and the fetials only carried it out. This seems to have been a standard practice. Thus, around 266 B.C. the aedilicians Q. Fabius and Cn. Apronius were ordered by the senate to be surrendered to Appolonia for striking ambassadors. The fetials carried out the order.[7] The fetials exercised their functions in various ways. They might be asked by the senate or elected official what was religiously proper to be done. Or as here they might simply be asked to perform the rituals following a decision of the senate.[8]

But they could also exercise jurisdiction directly, hearing cases. A text of Nonius, 529, quoting Varro is too precise in its language to admit of doubt:[9]

> The same [i.e., Varro] in book three: "If the ambassadors of any people were assaulted they determined that those who had done it, even if they were outstanding by reason of rank, should be surrendered to the state; and the twenty fetials who investigated these matters so gave judgment, and determined, and decided.[10]

The final words are legalese and denote either a judgment given in an actual case or the standard formulation. Probably it is to this jurisdiction that we should attribute the fetials' behavior when in 390 B.C. one of the Fabii clan, Quintus Ambustus, attacked a Gaul, thus violating a truce, breaking his oath, and fighting when a war had not been declared. Plutarch deals with the episode in two passages, one of which was quoted in chapter 1.[11] The other is more detailed for present purposes.

> *Camillus,* 18.1. When the senate convened in Rome, many denounced the Fabii, and especially the priests called *fetiales* were insistent in calling upon the senate in the name of all the gods to turn the curse of what had been done upon the one guilty man, and so to make expiation for the rest.
>
> These *fetiales* were instituted by Numa Pompilius, gentlest and justest of kings, to be the guardians of peace, as well as judges and determiners of the grounds on which war could justly be made.
>
> 2. The senate referred the matter to the people, and although the priests with one accord denounced Fabius, the multitude so scorned and mocked at religion as to appoint him military tribune, along with his brothers.

The senate's behavior, in taking the issue to the people, is not consistent with the notion that they sought a cautelary judgment from the fetials. The fetials gave judgment on their own account.

Much of the substance of Roman international law that relates to the *fetiales* has by now emerged incidentally, and it is perhaps convenient to deal with the remaining texts.

D.50.7.18(17). If anyone struck an ambassador of the enemy, he is thought to have so acted contrary to the law of all peoples (*or* of nations), because ambassadors are held to be sacred. And therefore if ambassadors of some people were with us and war was declared with them, the answer was that they remained free men: for this is proper for the law of nations. And therefore Quintus Mucius was accustomed to give the reply that he who struck an ambassador ought to be surrendered to the enemy whose ambassadors they were. The question arose whether, if the enemy did not accept him, he remained a Roman citizen. Some thought he did, others took the opposite view, because anyone whom the people had once ordered to be surrendered seemed to have been expelled from the state, just as happened when someone was interdicted from fire and water. This seems to have been the view of Publius Mucius. The question arose most notably in the case of Hostilius Mancinus whom the Numantini did not accept when surrendered to them. However, a law was later passed about him, so that he would be a Roman citizen, and he is also said to have held the praetorship.[12]

Thus, a Roman formally ordered to be surrendered to the enemy ceased to be a Roman citizen. When the enemy refused to accept him—presumably believing that such surrender was no adequate recompense—it was disputed whether he remained a Roman citizen. Such disputes were common in a state that left much of the development of Roman law in the hands of private individuals, the jurists, who in that capacity had no state authority. In the famous instance of Hostilius Mancinus in 137 B.C., a statute was passed giving him citizenship in order to remove any doubt.[13]

For the Romans it also made a legal difference whether the war being waged was proper:

D.49.15.24 (Ulpian, book 1 of *Institutes*). The enemy are those on whom the Roman people has publicly declared war, or who have declared war on the Roman people. Others are called robbers or bandits. And, therefore, a person captured by robbers is not a slave of the robbers, nor has he need of *postliminium* [right of reentry]. But a person captured by the enemy, for instance by the Germans and Parthians, both is a slave of the enemy, and recovers his former status by *postliminium*.[14]

A Roman captured in a proper war ceased to be a citizen and at once became a foreign slave. If he returned to Rome in a way that was creditable to him, he regained his citizenship. Various, but not all, of his previous private law rights were restored to him by the doctrine of *postliminium*.

The role of the fetial priests is remarkably unreligious. The role of the pontiffs was to ensure the right relations between deities and men, especially leading political figures and even the state itself. In the absence of divine revelation, they developed a scientific and legalistic approach to sacred issues. They dealt with religious questions such as whether a vow could be for an uncertain sum of money, whether Cicero's house had properly been dedicated as a temple, whether a chapel in a temple could properly be dedicated to more than one deity, whether a body had been buried properly and religiously. They knew the wording and forms of prayer needed to make gods propitious, how to persuade the gods of a foreign city to desert it and come over to the Romans, and the flaws that would render a prayer inefficacious. They knew the proper form of a vow to win the favor of a god. Although the pontifical religion might say nothing on how to lead the moral life, it said a great deal on how men should conduct themselves toward the gods.[15]

But there is nothing like this is the fetial religion. The substantive content of the fetials' functions is entirely secular: the determination of a just war, the proper treatment of ambassadors, offenses against a state for which the surrender of offenders may be granted or demanded. The role of the fetials does not extend to seeking the favor of the gods for the Roman people or to warding off their anger.

To this analysis it may be objected that there is, indeed, a religious content in the use of an oath, breach of which is to result in divine punishment. But the end envisaged for the oath is entirely secular, the protection from breach of a treaty which itself has no religious content.[16]

Karl-Heinz Ziegler believes the sacred character of the *ius fetiale* cannot be disputed, and that a sacred input is a characteristic of early law.[17] But elsewhere I have disputed the input of religion into early Roman private law—the Twelve Tables, for instance, are remarkably secular[18]—and now I would not accept that the *ius fetiale* has a sacred character even though it is the responsibility of a priestly college. In fact, the problem is why priests are allotted these tasks at all—secular ambassadors, such as are found elsewhere, could also have performed these functions. And the fetials had no other religious function. The explanation, which I will develop more fully subsequently in this book, is that the *fetiales* were most likely a special creation of the Latins who were ethnically related (or, less likely, of other central Italian peoples related to each other), who had no common political institutions, but did share religious traditions, and were faced by powerful enemies. Advantage was taken of the shared religion to have priests as ambassadors whose real function was to preserve peace among the Latin peoples when conflicts of interest arose among them.

# Six

# Breaches of Faith
# and Manipulation

Oaths or quasi oaths were involved in the ceremonies both for declarations of war and treaty making. In the former, according to Livy, the fetial who claimed wrongfully and contrary to religion was not to enjoy his native land again. In the latter, the Romans who broke faith were to be struck more powerfully by Jupiter than the sacrificed pig was struck by the fetial.[1]

Further light may be shed on the oath in these contexts by other texts. Polybius describes the oath binding the treaty with the Carthaginians in 279 B.C.:

> 3.25.6. The oaths they had to swear were as follows. In the case of the first treaty the Carthaginians swore by their ancestral gods and the Romans, following an old custom, by Juppiter Lapis and, in the case of this latter treaty, by Mars and Quirinus. 7. The oath by Juppiter Lapis is as follows. The man who is swearing to the treaty takes in his hand a stone, and when he has sworn in the name of the state, he says, 8. "If I abide by this my oath may all good be mine, but if I do otherwise in thought or act, let all other men dwell safe in their own countries under their own laws and in possession of their own substance, temples, and tombs, and may I alone be cast forth, even as this stone," and so saying he throws the stone from his hand.

No mention is made of a sacrifice of a pig but the priest hurls a stone. According to this, it is the priest personally who is to suffer the penalty even though he swore in the name of the state. Throwing of a stone as part of the ceremony of an oath appears also in Festus, s.v. *lapidem silicem.*

> Those about to swear by Jupiter held a stone of flint, saying these words, "If I knowingly deceive, then may Jupiter throw me out of my property, keeping the city and the citadel safe, as I cast this stone.[2]

No context is given for this oath, but it would seem to be a public occasion in view of *salva urbe arceque*. The maker of the oath is to be punished for his breach of faith but the city and the citadel are to be kept safe.

The breach of an oath incurred the wrath of the gods. Indeed, the gods were even more entitled to inflict punishment than the other nation that was injured. The gods could be expected to take revenge:

> Livy, 8.39.10. After all that had gone before, this defeat so broke the spirit of the Samnites that the murmur was heard in all their councils that it was indeed no wonder if, having undertaken an impious war and contrary to treaty, and with the gods deservedly more hostile than men, they met with no success. This war would have to be expiated and attoned for with a heavy price. 11. The only question was whether they should offer atonement with the blood of the guilty few or of the innocent multitude. Some dared even to name those responsible for the war.[3]

The wrath of the gods might be diminished if those who broke the treaty offered to make amends. Indeed, if the injured nation rejected the overtures of those who broke the treaty, the wrath of the gods might be turned against it.[4] Presumably it is in this context that we must place the instances where a Roman who is surrendered is refused by the enemy: the enemy does not deem the reparation to be sufficient.

In any event, faith ought to be kept in an oath with a public enemy.

> Cicero, *De officiis*, 3.29.107. But there is even law relating to war, and fidelity to an oath must often be kept with an enemy. For when an

oath is so sworn that one understands in one's own mind that it should be performed, then it must be kept. But if it is not so understood, then if it is not performed there is no perjury. For instance, if you do not bring the price agreed for your life to pirates, this is no fraud, not even if you do not do what you swore to do. For a pirate is not included in the number of lawful enemies but is the common enemy of all. Nor with him should there be any common faith or oath. 108. For swearing what is false is not perjury but when you swear "upon your conscience" as these words are used according to our custom, and do not perform, that is perjury. For Euripides aptly writes, "I swore with my tongue, I bear an unsworn mind." But Regulus had no right to disturb with perjury the terms and agreements of war made with an enemy. For the war was being waged with a lawful enemy, and to regulate this we have all the fetial law, and many common laws. If this were not the case, the senate would never have surrendered distinguished men, bound, to the enemy.[5]

Cicero seems to be saying that no perjury is involved when one does not keep an oath made with a common criminal in order to save one's life. On the other hand, one should keep an oath made to an enemy provided it was made with no mental reservations. In fact, it was standard, as we have already seen, to insert express words, excluding such reservations.[6]

It was an accepted part of Roman religion that the strict formalities and ceremonies could be manipulated in order to produce a desired result. Good faith was not always requisite provided strict legalistic, formalistic reasoning could give the Roman what he wanted. Thus, to avoid seeing unfavorable signs, a Roman general might have himself carried to the battlefield in a closed litter.[7] To ensure that the sacred chickens dropped grain from their beaks— a propitious sign—the *pullarii*, the keepers of the sacred chickens, who attended on the magistrates (and presumably also on the augurs), might starve them first so that they pecked greedily.[8] Words might be given an unexpected and unintended but possible meaning.[9] It is on this account that we find such precautionary clauses as that in the treaty in Livy, 1.24.7, "as these terms are today most correctly understood."

Bad faith in war was not in itself unpleasing to the gods provided no specific religious obligation was broken. The clearest case of manipulation occurs after the Caudine Fork disaster when the guarantors of peace are being surrendered, bound, to the Samnites.

> Livy, 9.5.10. As the fetial was saying these words, Postumius thrust his knee into the other's thigh with as much force as he could: and he declared in a clear voice that he was a Samnite citizen, that he had violated the envoy contrary to the law of nations. On that basis, the Romans would wage war more justly.[10]

Here lies the manipulation. By his surrender, as would be the case by being taken captive, the Roman ex-consul ceased to be a Roman citizen.[11] Instead, he belonged to the Samnites, as a slave.[12] Thus, his assault on the Roman fetial is a Samnite assault and makes the ensuing war a just Roman war. An assault upon a priest and ambassador is a breach of a religious obligation. It makes no difference that Postumius was acting as a loyal Roman, that he hated the Samnites, and that his purpose was, after Roman treachery, to give color to a Roman claim to wage a just war.

# Seven

## Surrender of an Enemy City

Surprisingly, perhaps, the formulas for surrendering a city, on which we are well informed, give particular insights into the nature of fetial law.

In the reign of Tarquinius Priscus (616–579 B.C.), the Romans inflicted a severe defeat upon the Sabines. Tarquinius sent the prisoners and booty to Rome and, in fulfillment of a vow to Vulcan, he made a huge pile of the captured arms and burned them.[1] The Sabines took to the field again and were again routed. Then:

> Livy, 1.38.1. Collatia and whatever land there was on this side of Collatia was taken from the Sabines. Egerius, the son of the king's brother was left garrisoning Collatia. I believe the Collatini surrendered themselves with this formula. 2. The king asked: "Are you the legates and the spokesmen sent by the Collatine people in order that you surrender yourselves and the Collatine people?" "We are." "Is the Collatine people its own master?" "It is." "Do you surrender the Collatine people, the city, fields, water, boundaries, shrines, utensils, all things divine and human into the dominion [*dicio*] of me and of the Roman people?" "We make the surrender." "I receive it." 3. On the conclusion of the Sabine war, Tarquinius returned to Rome, and triumphed.[2]

A second formulation is found on a recently discovered bronze tablet, which can be dated, from the names of the consuls, to 104 B.C. It was found in the district of Alcántara in the province of Cáceres in Spain, and at the relevant date the area would have been under the rule of the Roman in charge of Hispania Ulterior.[3] The tablet is incomplete, the right side having been broken off. I follow the reconstruction of Dieter Nörr.[4] His alternative suggestions for lost words I have placed in parentheses:

> In the consulate of Gaius Marius and Gaius Flavius. The people of the Seano[ surrendered itself and its belongings to Lucius Caesius, son of Gaius, general, and after he received them into his trust (dominion), he referred to the council the issue of what they decided should be commanded to them. On the instruction of the council he commanded that they surrender their arms and hostages (deserters), captives, the horses and mares they had captured. All these they gave. Then Lucius Caesius, son of Gaius, general, ordered them to be free, and he returned the fields and buildings and laws and everything also that they had before they surrendered and which were extant, for so long as the Roman people and senate wished, and on that matter he ordered them to send legates to go to Rome. Crenus, son of X, and Arco, son of Canto, were the legates.[5]

Nörr observes that in this type of *deditio,* of a community to the Romans, a connection with the *ius fetiale* is doubtful.[6] But I believe one can go further and claim that the fetials and the *ius fetiale* were not involved in the surrender of a city. The point is not that we have no evidence that they were involved, but that we have two precise formulations that show they were not. In the first, that of Livy, that ostensibly goes back to the regal period, the spokesman for the Romans is the king himself. There is no sign of the fetials. Yet in Livy's parallel passages giving the form of declarations of war and treaty making, there do appear the fetials. Moreover, this surrender is of Collatia, a Latin habitation, and, as we saw in chapter 1, we would expect the Collatini also to have fetials, and to use them, if they were appropriate. Yet their representatives are not named as fetials but as legates and spokesmen. In the second formulation, the Spanish Seano surrenders itself again to the Roman general, not to fetials. Certainly, Seano in Spain would have had no fetials, but, as we will see in chapter 8, tradition ensured that the Romans continued to use the fetial ritual even though there were no such priests on the other side. Again, Dionysius of Halicarnassus at 2.72 purports to give an account of the many and great functions of the fetials. He describes the declarations of war, treaty making, and the surrender of individuals. But nowhere does he ascribe to the fetials a role in the surrender of a city.

In fact, there is little in common between the *deditio* of individuals and that of a community. The first and most striking difference relates to the point of time in the whole process when the surrender occurs. The surrender of individuals is related to the declaration of war, and is a preliminary either to war or the avoidance of war. There are two possible scenarios. Either the surrender occurs on the demand of the fetials for restitution, in the run up to the declaration of war. Or the surrendering nation makes the surrender even before restitution is claimed, on the basis that by this act it is righting the wrong. In contrast, *deditio* of a community has nothing to do with the declaration of war. The war has been declared before, has been fought, and victory obtained, and now the vanquished are making formal surrender. The *deditio,* or request therefor, of individuals was part of the procedure for avoiding war or setting up a just cause of war in order to initiate a lawsuit with the gods as judges. It should further be observed that there is no intervention or involvement of gods in the surrender of a community.

For whatever reason, and possible reasons will be examined subsequently in this chapter, surrender of a community was outside the scope of the *fetiales,* and did not seem to involve priests at all.[7]

The texts indicate that there were two kinds of surrender of a community, *deditio in dicionem* 'surrender into the dominion' and *deditio in fidem* 'surrender in trust', although modern scholars tend to think the distinction more rhetorical than judicial.[8] To come to a just estimation of this we should first look at an element in the *deditio* of an individual already considered in chapter 4. That *deditio* is a parallel to noxal surrender in private law. When a slave (or son) without authorization committed a wrong, the head of a family could free himself from all obligation by surrendering the wrongdoer to the victim. Likewise in *deditio* of an individual, the state was released from all obligation by the surrender. And in *deditio* of an individual, the wording used by Livy is that appropriate to the noxal surrender of private law. Of course, in the *deditio* of a community, the surrender is not that of dependents in another's power. Indeed, we saw from Livy, 1.38.2, that the surrendering people had to be in its own control, *in sua potestate*. Here we have another reminiscence of private law. For the formal surrender of a warring city to the Romans, it is not enough that it be vanquished. The city authorities have to declare that it was not in the power of another state. Otherwise the city would not lawfully be able to give itself into the power, *potestas,* of the Romans.

This correspondence will prove useful for possible variations in the *deditio* of a people. Valerius Maximus records the surrender of Falerii after it had taken up arms against the Romans in 241 B.C. in the first Punic War:

> 6.5.1. The same state, rebelling several times and always bruised in lost battles, at last was compelled to surrender itself to the consul, Quintus Lutatius. The Roman people wished to treat it with ferocity but, after the people was taught by Papirius (by whose hand at the order of the consul the words of the surrender were written down) that the Falisci had committed themselves not to the power [*potestas*] but to the trust [*fides*] of the Romans, it laid aside all its anger with a quiet mind.[9]

In his turn, Livy records a speech of the Gallic legates before the Roman senate in 183 B.C. They said:

> 39.54.6. . . . Recently Marcus Claudius had sent a messenger that he would wage war with them unless they surrendered. 7. Preferring a certain even if unattractive peace to the uncertainties of war, they had surrendered themselves into the trust [*dedidisse se in fidem*] rather than into the power [*in potestatem*] of the Roman people.[10]

Without doubt, Valerius Maximus is claiming that there is a substantive difference between *deditio in fidem* and *deditio in potestatem* and that this has important consequences for the way the Romans can with propriety treat the surrendered people. This difference results from the wording of the surrender, which seems to have been written down. Valerius Maximus does not treat the difference as rhetorical but legal. Also against the notion of a rhetorical invention is the fact that one would have to claim that Livy had stumbled upon the same notion for a similar rhetorical effect.

In this instance, too, a private law analogue may provide clarification. *Mancipatio* was the formal ceremony in early and classical law for transferring ownership of those important kinds of things known as *res mancipi*: slaves, cattle, horses, mules, asses, land in Italy, and rustic servitudes.[11] A variant form of wording in which the same objects could be transferred to the faith and trust (*fide et fiduciae* or *fidi fiduciae causa*) of the recipient created the form of real security known as *fiducia*.[12] Ownership of the objects was transferred to the creditor, but only in trust. He could not use the property, and had to return it in certain circumstances, namely when the debt was paid. This *fiducia* is significant here.

The situation, I suggest, was somewhat similar when a people surrendered itself *in fidem* of the Romans. The Romans cannot lawfully treat it just as they like. They cannot simply savage the surrendered Falisci. The episode recorded by Livy is even more explicative. The wrong the Gauls had committed was to cross the Alps and settle in an uninhabited area.[13] After their surrender, the senate's response was to order them to recross the Alps, but also to give them back all their property.[14]

The absence of any role for the fetials in accepting the surrender of an enemy city reveals the true nature of the *ius fetiale*. The fetials are nothing more nor less than the official state emissaries of peace; and, at that, originally and primarily emissaries of peace among the Latins (or some other central Italian peoples). Peace is good in itself, and all the more so when it is maintained among kinfolk. It is noteworthy that Janus Quirinus is invoked in the declaration of war in Livy, 1.32.10. That unified god is, indeed, otherwise attested but, when the gods are treated as separate, Janus is the god of beginnings, and Quirinus is the god of the army at peace.[15] The fetials are thus responsible for the ritual surrounding the making of treaties, which are primarily geared toward peace. They are also responsible for declarations of war. But not only are the fetials to ensure that the war is just, the declaration of war is itself represented as a last resort. The fetials are to demand reparation for wrongs, the demands being repeated three times at ten-day intervals. Only then, if reparation is not made, will the king or senate determine upon war. Significantly, the *pater patratus,* when demanding restitution, calls down the wrath of Jupiter upon himself if his demands are unjust. He does not call down the wrath of Jupiter on the other people if they refuse restitution.[16] The cry is not for vengeance. In this search for peace, the fetials may demand the surrender to them of individuals who have transgressed against them. The surrender to the other people of Romans who wronged them is simply the other side of this coin.

But the fetials have no role to play in the conduct of a war. They will fulfill the ritual requirements for a peace treaty, but they do not accept the surrender of a defeated community. If the war is going badly, the fetials will not reconsider whether, perhaps, the war is unjust. Instead, the *augures* will try to discover whether the auspices of the commanding general were in order, and others will look for signs and portents to indicate what has gone wrong, and what is to be done.[17] If a general wishes to secure the favor of a god, he may offer to make a vow. It is the task of the *pontifices,* not of the fetials, to determine whether a particular vow has been or can be properly made.[18] When the tutelary deities had been persuaded to abandon an enemy city, the Romans might devote and consecrate the city and its army to destruction. Here, too, the ritual formula was not entrusted to the fetials: it could be pronounced only by the dictator or top general.[19]

# Eight

# Survival and Change

etial law was fundamentally unsuitable for declarations
of war and treaty making for a city on its way to world
domination. In its pure form, the system required par-
ticipation of the other state's fetials, but they did not
exist outside of central Italy. Hence, fetial law should
have been inappropriate beyond this area. A system that involved
the plucking of the *verbena* from the citadel was also unsuitable for
wars to be carried on at any distance from the city. The system was,
indeed, devised to keep peace among the Latins. We have already
seen that changes occurred with time, and that *legati et oratores* 'ambassadors and spokesmen' might replace the *fetiales*.

Still, war and religion were central elements in Roman life.
Human beings tend not to be overly inventive: ideas and procedures that have outlived their setting in life continue in being. And
there may be little in human experience as traditional and resilient
as religion. The system might be unsuitable and subject to great
strain, might eventually even break down, without disappearing
altogether.[1] This chapter concerns the remains of the system once
it could no longer operate properly.

If we may trust Livy, the Roman system was operating in
changed circumstances in 322 B.C. The Samnites had broken a

truce, then suffered grievous defeats, and were blaming those responsible for the war:

> 8.39.12. One name above all, that of Brutulus Papius, could be heard, and all agreed on it. He was a nobleman and powerful, and without doubt the breaker of the most recent truce. 13. The praetors were compelled to refer his case and they issued a decree that Brutulus Papius should be surrendered to the Romans and with him, all the Roman booty and the prisoners should be sent to Rome; and also whatever had been sought by the fetials should be restored according to law and religion. 14. The fetials proceeded to Rome in accordance with this resolution, taking the lifeless body of Brutulus: for he by a voluntary death removed himself from shame and torture. 15. But the Romans accepted nothing of these things apart from the prisoners and whatever from the booty could be recognized as theirs. The surrender of other things had no validity. The dictator celebrated a triumph by decree of the senate.[2]

So far as our evidence goes, the Samnites had no fetials.[3] But they recognized the fetials as the proper representatives of the Romans. Hence, when they decided to make reparation for the broken treaty, they surrendered their leading wrongdoer's body, their prisoners of war and other booty, and other things to the fetials to take to Rome. The Romans refused to accept anything they did not recognize as theirs: that is, they wished to impose harder terms. From this we also see that just as the fetials could not decide on a war, but only declare that the war would be just, so also they did not decide that reparations should be accepted.

The breakdown of the fetial rite in declarations of war is most dramatically seen in the Roman war with Pyrrus, king of Epirus in the early third century B.C. His kingdom lay across the Adriatic, hence it was not practicable to throw a spear across his boundaries. A soldier of Pyrrhus, who had been captured and made a prisoner of war, was forced to buy a piece of land near the temple of Bellona,[4] and this land was then declared to be enemy ground. Bellona, Roman war goddess, had a temple vowed to her in 296 B.C. by Appius Claudius Caecus in the war against the combined Etruscan and Samnite forces;[5] and shortly thereafter the temple was built near the old altar of Mars, and the later Circus Flaminius.

Before this temple stood the *columna bellica* 'war column'. From this column was thrown the lance of the fetials into what was designated as enemy territory. The whole procedure is reminiscent of the use of fictions in Roman private law. Thereafter this became the standard practice whenever it was not easily possible to throw the lance into enemy territory:[6]

> Servius, *In Vergilii Aeneidon libris* 9.52. . . . Thirty-three days after they had demanded restitution from the enemy, the fetials threw the spear. Subsequently when in the time of Pyrrhus the Romans were about to wage war against an overseas enemy, and found no place where they might perform this solemnity of declaring war through the fetials, they devised this scheme that one of Pyrrhus's soldiers was captured, and they compelled him to buy land in the Circus Flaminius so that they might carry out the law of declaring war as if in enemy territory. Later in that place, in front of the temple of Bellona a column was consecrated. Varro in his *Calenus* says this: "When the leaders were first about to enter enemy territory, for the sake of an omen they first threw a spear into that territory, to capture a place for their camp."[7]

> Festus, s.v. Bellona. Bellona was the name of the goddess of wars. Before her temple was a little column which was called *bellica* ['warlike'], over which they threw a spear when war was declared.[8]

Some modern scholars discount this story: indeed, it is used as part of the argument that the whole fetial lore is a later invention of the Romans.[9] The observations on which this rejection are based are acute and accurate, even if one believes (as I do) that the conclusion is unwarranted. Thus, Wiedemann says:

> (a) The story implies that fighting had already been going on, or the soldier could not have been captured. Should we think of the Romans as assuming that such fighting had not been in accordance with fetial law?[10] (b) A non citizen (let alone a *hostis*) cannot buy land. Readers would have to assume that the captive had first been manumitted as a Roman citizen; in which case he was no longer a *hostis*. (c) The Romans were actually at war with Tarentum, not Epirus (whose king appeared on the scene as a hired ally of Tarentum). *Fetiales* could have cast a ceremonial lance at Tarentine soil without difficulty had they felt so inclined.[11]

Yes, all this is correct, but the objections to drawing conclusions from the observations are twofold.

First, the observations fail to take into account the nature of general legal logic in making inventive use of formalities. One Roman example from *mancipatio* will serve as an illustration. *Mancipatio* was a formal ceremony for transferring ownership of the small class of important things known as *res mancipi*. In the presence of the transferor, five adults who were there as witnesses and another who held bronze scales, the transferee grasped the object with one hand, struck the scales with a piece of copper, and declared in formal language that he had bought the thing. *Mancipatio* operated as an immediate transfer, and no physical delivery was necessary, whereas for objects that were not *res mancipi* actual physical delivery was needed to transfer ownership. *Mancipatio* came to be used abusively for many purposes, including marriage and adoption,[12] but here we need consider only its use to make a will since the form of that has been already described in chapter 2. In this instance, the recipient who spoke the formula acquired no rights in the testator's property, the testator remained owner until his death, and at that point of time under this will the heir automatically became owner even of things that were not *res mancipi*.[13] Thus, in this one instance, three important features of *mancipatio* were subverted. The point I want to make is that with changing times, Roman creativity could make new use of existing institutions to reach particular goals and in doing this they did not feel constrained by strict logic.[14]

The second point is that the fetial rite had by this time lost its function: to preserve, if possible, peace among the Latins who also had fetials and had a shared religion. Still, some formality had to be used to declare war. In the absence of anything else, it was natural to use a modified fetial rite, without overmuch concern for legal technicalities.[15] On this approach, one need not hold that in such circumstances the Romans still believed that a just cause was needed for a just war: performance of the modified formalities may have been sufficient.

Although *fetiales* might still be used, negotiations with a foreign power leading even to the declaration of war were, in general, entrusted to senatorial legates.[16] The most famous episode is from 218 B.C. The Romans had voted for a war with Carthage.[17] Then:

> Livy, 21.18.1. After these arrangements had been made, in order that before they made war everything should be properly done, they sent older legates, Quintus Fabius, Marcus Livius, Lucius Aemilius, Gaius Licinius, and Quintus Baebius, to demand of the Carthaginians whether Hannibal had attacked Saguntum with the approval of the state.[18]

Even more significant, Sallust's account of the Jugurthine War of the late second century B.C. reveals that, without the *fetiales* and without the religious rites, Roman ambassadors followed the same steps in declaring war.[19] Tradition dies hard.

The treaty-making functions of the fetials in fact survived their departure from declarations of war.[20] One prime source of our information for later times is the famous grammarian, Marcus Terentius Varro (116–27 B.C.), who fought on the side of Pompey in Spain in 49 B.C., was restored to favor by Julius Caesar in 47, and appointed keeper of the future public library. After Caesar was murdered, Marcus Antonius outlawed Varro in 43, but he escaped death. His *De lingua latina* was published before Cicero's death, probably also in 43. His account of the fetials ought to reflect something of the conditions of these times:

> 5.86. The *fetiales* were so called because they were in charge of public faith [*fides publica*] between peoples. For by them it was brought about that a war would be a just war, and then ended, so that the faith of peace might be constituted in a treaty. Some of them were sent before war was declared to demand restitution, and by them even now a treaty [*foedus*] is made, which Ennius says was pronounced *fidus*.[21]

Varro's concern is with etymology, fanciful or not, and he had no religious or political message. He represents the use of fetials as obsolete in declarations of war but still current in treaty making.

This argument from Varro should not be considered doubtful because of Cicero, *De legibus*, 2.9.21.

> The fetials shall be the judges and messengers of treaties, peace, war, truces, and ambassadors. They shall make the determination with regard to war.[22]

Cicero is constructing an outline of the ideal laws. This outline, in fact, corresponds closely in general to Roman law. But this passage shows at the most that these functions had been the Roman role for the fetials. It does not necessarily reflect current practice but only what Cicero, in his moralizing mode, would like to see.

Suetonius represents the emperor Claudius as continuing to use the fetial rite for treaty making:

> *Divus Claudius*, 25.5. . . . When he concluded a treaty with foreign kings, he sacrificed a pig in the forum according to the ancient fetial rites. Yet this and all his other similar acts, and much that he did in his reign, were at the instigation of his wives and freedmen, since he almost always acted in accordance with their interests and wishes.[23]

Suetonius writes of this as a peculiarity of Claudius, and that the rite was otherwise long obsolete. We may regard his behavior here as another instance of his famed antiquarianism.

If the fetial rite for declaring war was obsolete in the time of Varro, as has been argued, it was renewed by Octavian (later Augustus) in 32 B.C. against Antony.

> Cassius Dio, 50.4.4. This caused the Romans in their indignation to believe that the other reports in circulation were also true, to the effect that if Antony should prevail, he would bestow their city upon Cleopatra and transfer the seat of power to Egypt. 2. And they became so angry at this that all, not only Antony's enemies or those who were not siding with either man, but even his most intimate friends, censured him severely; for in their consternation at what was read and in their eagerness to counteract Caesar's suspicion of them, they spoke in the same way as the rest. 3. They deprived him of the consulship to which he had been previously elected, and of all his authority in general. They did not, to be sure, declare him an enemy in so many words, because they were afraid his adherents would also have to be regarded in the light of enemies, in case they should not abandon him; but by this action they showed their attitude more plainly than by any words. 4. For they voted to the men arrayed on his side pardon and praise if they would abandon him, and declared war outright upon Cleopatra, put on their military cloaks as if he were close at hand, 5. and went to the temple of Bellona, where they performed through Caesar as *fetialis* all the rites preliminary to war in the customary fashion. These proceed-

ings were nominally directed against Cleopatra, but really against Antony. 5.1. For she had enslaved him so absolutely that she persuaded him to act as gymnasiarch to the Alexandrians; and she was called "queen" and "mistress" by him, had Roman soldiers in her bodyguard, and all of these inscribed her name upon their shields. 2. She used to frequent the marketplace with him, joined him in the management of festivals and in the hearing of lawsuits, and rode with him even in the cities, or else was carried in a chair while Antony accompanied her on foot along with her eunuchs. He also termed his headquarters "the palace," sometimes wore an oriental dagger at his belt, dressed in a manner not in accordance with the customs of his native land, 3. and let himself be seen even in public upon a gilded couch or a chair of that kind.

We may well give credit to Cassius Dio's story that the procedure, though technically against Cleopatra, was really directed toward Antony. Octavian had a political purpose in appearing as a fetial: to make Antony a foreign enemy.

Marcus Aurelius, as late as A.D. 178 used the same ceremony for the war against the Marcomanni:

Cassius Dio, 72.33.2. . . . "As for us," he said, in addressing the senate, "we are so far from possessing anything of our own that even the house in which we live is yours." 3. Then, after making this speech and after hurling the bloody spear, which was kept in the temple of Bellona, into what was supposed to be the enemy's territory (as I have heard men who were present relate), he set out; and he gave a large force to Paternus and sent him to the scene of the fighting. The barbarians held out for the entire day, but were all cut down by the Romans; 4. and Marcus was saluted *imperator* for the tenth time.

The latest reference to the fetials is in Ammianus Marcellinus, for the year A.D. 359:

19.2.6. Scarcely had Grumbates hurled the bloodstained spear in the custom of his people and of our fetial priest, than the army, clashing its weapons, rushed to the walls, and at once the tearful tempest of war grew fiercer, with the cavalry advancing at full speed as they hurried to the fight with eagerness in all of them. Our men resisted bravely and determinedly.[24]

Grumbates was king of the Chionitae and an enemy of Rome. Hurling a spear over enemy walls as a sign of battle was scarcely unique to the Romans. The passage is no evidence that any trace of Roman fetial rites survived.

Long before this, the secularization of treaty making was well brought out by the jurist Gaius in his *Institutes,* which were written around A.D. 161.[25] Writing about the private law contract of *stipulatio,* he records that the verb *spondere* can only be used for it by Roman citizens.[26] Then he proceeds:

> G.3.94. Hence it is said that in one case a peregrine can also be bound by this word, namely if our emperor puts the question about peace in this way to the ruler of some peregrine people: "Do you solemnly promise there will be peace?" Or our emperor is asked in the same way. But this statement is oversubtle, because, if anything is done contrary to the agreement, an action is not brought on the stipulation, but the matter is pursued by the law of war.[27]

Gaius is being properly fastidious.[28] The treaty, though cast in the form of a stipulation, is not a stipulation because it does not give rise to the action appropriate to a *stipulatio.* Indeed, he is saying, there is no action at law. When he says "the matter is pursued by the law of war," he means only that when a peace treaty is broached, the only recourse is to war.

# Nine

# War, Law, and Religion

The argument to this point may be summarized. The *ius fetiale*—and *ius* 'law' is accurate terminology—was a wonderful creation of the Latins (or possibly some other central Italian people). Which community was responsible cannot be established. The whole purpose of the *ius fetiale* was the preservation of peace among an ethnically and linguistically related group of states that also were faced by hostile neighbors. Latin communities had no organized political relationship, but they had common religious ties.[1] They traded on these to set up, in each community, a body of priests who could use a shared religious tradition to keep peace and, if all else failed, to declare a just war. A few neighboring communities followed suit. The war had supposedly to be just from a substantive aspect, but in keeping with the nature of Roman (and, presumably, Latin) religion, formalities were central. If, despite all, war had to be declared, gods were called upon to act as judges: their role in this was to decide that the war was just. No vows were made to them, nor were supplications; for the *ius fetiale* the gods were, and were meant to be, neutral arbiters.

It is deeply revealing that such a system does not seem to have existed elsewhere in the Western world.[2] It is a system geared to a very particular situation: related communities with a shared religion but no joint political structure, and who had differences of interest and neighboring enemies.[3] These are the realities that underlie the famous duel between the Roman brothers Horatii and the Alba Longan brothers Curiati.

War had already been declared between Rome and Alba Longa, and the armies were in line of battle. Mettius Fufetius, the Alban leader, suggested a conference before fighting began. The Alban said:

> Livy, 1.23.7. "Wrongs and failure to return the property demanded in accordance with the treaty, I seem to have heard our king Cluilius declare to be the cause of this war, and I do not doubt, Tullus, that you make the same claim. But if the truth rather than sophistries are to be spoken, it is greed for dominion that excites two related and neighboring peoples to arms. 8. Whether rightly or wrongly I do not judge. That will have been the decision of him who undertook the war. The Albans simply made me the general for waging the war. But this is what I want to warn you, Tullus. How great the Etruscan power is that surrounds us and especially you, you know better to the extent that you are closer. Their strength is great on land, very great on sea. 9. You should remember that as soon as you give the signal for battle, these two battle lines will be a spectacle, so that they may attack when we, both the victor and the vanquished, are tired and exhausted. So, if the gods love us, since we are not content with certain liberty but are advancing to the chance of dominion or servitude, let us devise some way by which may be decided who controls the other without a great disaster and much bloodshed of both peoples.[4]

Thus, the way devised was for victory to be decided by a duel between champions—in the event, the Horatii and the Curiatii. The victory of the former resulted in Rome's domination of Alba Longa. In this particular instance the *fetiales* failed in their purpose. War was declared. But then, a subsequent attempt was still made to keep the peace, and this reveals the fetials' real function. For present purposes it makes little difference whether we regard the duel as a true, historical event; or as a legend invented to explicate the role intended for the *fetiales*; or even as simply a legend. In any eventuality the nature of fetial law clearly emerges.

The functions of the fetials correspond very closely to those of modern ambassadors: they demand reparation from foreign states for wrongs; they formally ratify treaties; they present the formal declaration of war; but they do not accept the formal surrender of the foreign state. But the fetials, in theory at least, had to ensure that the war was just; ambassadors simply follow the instructions of their government. And, in pursuit of their functions, the fetials as priests were in direct contact with the gods. The connection of the fetials with justice and the deities results naturally from their origins.

Priests rather than mere ambassadors were chosen for this role partly to increase the solemnity but mainly because it was above all in religion that the Latins had a shared tradition. Yet the priests could not simply be the *pontifices* because the *pontifices* had a different role: to keep or establish the right relations and favorable relations with the deities. In contrast, for the tasks facing and assigned to the *fetiales,* the gods had to be strictly neutral.

But Rome expanded beyond Latium and early had contact with other peoples. The *ius fetiale* in this context was inappropriate. Rome did not share a religious tradition with these peoples, who also did not have *fetiales*. The system broke down in all meaningful senses.[5] But tradition, as is its nature, prevailed. No other system replaced the *ius fetiale*. But, on the one hand, formalities were needed, especially for a declaration of war. The substantive just causes that underlay the declaration of war disappeared or at least fell into the background. The ritual for declaring war, in the absence of fetials on the other side, was transformed. Fetial rites, transmogrified according to legal logic, were retained for some time for declarations of war, but then they did disappear. For political purposes they were reinstated by Octavian. For long, though, the *fetiales* remained the formal treaty makers. But the religious heart of the system had gone. In reality, and often in practice, Roman fetials were replaced by ambassadors.

In the wider context of the Republic, at least until near the end of the second century B.C., the Romans regarded themselves as the most religious people in the world.[6] The nature of Roman literary sources is such that we do not have direct evidence on how they regarded themselves in earlier times. But the overwhelming probability is that religious observances were at least as strict in the regal period and earlier Republic.

Their reputation among foreigners was also of extreme religiosity. The classic statement is from the Greek chronicler of the Roman rise to world power, Polybius, who was born around 200 B.C. and died after 118.

> 6.56.6. But the quality in which the Roman state is most distinctly superior is, in my opinion, the nature of their religious convictions. 7. I believe that the very thing which among other people is an object of reproach, I mean superstition, is what maintains the Roman state. 8. These matters are clothed in such formalities and are introduced into their public and private life to such an extent that nothing could exceed it. This is a fact that will surprise many.[7]

In fact, this ascription of extreme religiosity to the Romans was such a commonplace that, later, Christian authors, such as Augustine[8] and Tertullian, poke fun at it. Thus, Tertullian, writing around A.D. 197:

> *Apologeticus*, 25.2. Since, however, mention of the Roman name has come up, I may not shirk the encounter challenged by the presumption of those who claim that the Romans have been raised to such a high point of grandeur as to hold the whole world as a reward for their outstanding religious attitude; and that their gods are so much gods that those persons flourish beyond all others who, beyond all others, render them their due. 3. Of course this reward has been paid by the Roman gods out of gratitude. Sterculus and Mutunus and Larentina extended their empire. For I would not suppose foreign gods would have wished to favor an alien race rather than their own, and to transfer to men from across the sea their native soil in which they were born, reared, ennobled, and buried.[9]

Sterculus, the god of dung,[10] Mutunus, the god of sexual intercourse,[11] and Larentina (or Accia Larentia), the foster-mother of Romulus and Remus, and who was reputed to be promiscuous,[12] are listed as native Roman gods, and given ironically as typical gods who raised Rome to its greatness. These and the very many other gods were of little significance, especially for the state religion, and only a hostile witness could claim they had a role in Rome's greatness. Indeed, such minor gods are missing from the field of war.[13] Still, in general their number indicates that for the Romans the divine is everywhere. And the passage of Tertullian shows the Roman belief that their greatness was due to their religiosity. The passage has no point otherwise.

In one sense this religiosity of the Romans is astounding. Although the religion had, like the Latin language, its roots in the Indo-European past, Roman state religion very early lost its mythology. The gods became depersonalized; the major deities had no history and no adventures. It became, at an early stage, a religion of observance, not of belief or theology.[14] Moreover, the state religion was not concerned with how its adherents should lead the moral life. From his Christian standpoint, Augustine puts the question why the Roman gods did not lay down laws of moral conduct. He said, "It would certainly appear proper that the care shown by the worshippers for the gods' rites be matched by the gods' concern for their behavior."[15]

Rather, state religion became restricted to a particular context. It became a matter of keeping man—especially man in his public function—in proper contact with the gods. The functions of the priests were to ensure that ceremonies were correctly and formalistically carried out in every detail. They had to ensure, for example, that meetings of the senate or *comitia* were opened with prayers said according to the fixed and rigid formulas. They had to see to it that the days on which such assemblies met or on which the praetor made pronouncements were auspicious. They were, in this way, responsible for the calendar. They also had to make sure that each sacrifice was carried out precisely in the way acceptable to the gods. They dictated to state officials what was religiously proper in the conduct of business, including the business of war. State religion was very important, but it became confined to its context. The main functions of the priests became, from a modern perspective, legal.[16]

This legalism is revealing, because in their secular life also the Romans have been the most legalistic of all people.[17] It is impossible to award priorities. There is no way to tell whether Roman religion became legalistic because of the Roman fascination with law, which is marked as far back as history records, or whether it was the character of Roman religion, which appears to us to be so legalistic, which inspired in the Romans a fascination with law. Because the most prominent men in the state were active in both spheres, it is probable that attitudes in one fed upon attitudes in the other.

What at least is certain is that Roman legal reasoning was based upon an internal logic that removed it, to a considerable extent, from immediate societal concerns.[18] One example, and only one example, need be given here to illustrate the approach.[19] The text, D.40.1.6, comes from Alfenus Varus who was active in the last century of the Republic.[20]

> A slave had bargained money for his freedom, and he gave the money to his owner. The owner died before he manumitted the slave, and in his will he ordered that he be free, and he left him a legacy of his *peculium.* He asked whether or not his patron's heirs were obliged to return the money that he had given to his owner in return for freedom. [The jurist] replied, if after he had received the money, the owner had entered it in his accounts as his money, it immediately ceased to be part of the *peculium;* but if, in the meantime, until he manumitted him, he had recorded it as due to the slave, it appeared to be part of the *peculium* and the heirs were bound to restore it to him now that he was freed.[21]

Roman slaves could own no property, but it was common for an owner to allow a slave a fund, the *peculium,* which the slave could deal with as if it were his own. The *peculium,* of course, belonged to the owner. But there were various circumstances, such as the one in this text, where the extent of the *peculium* would be externally and objectively assessed. When owners freed slaves by will, they frequently also bequeathed them a legacy of the *peculium.* In this instance an owner allowed the slave a *peculium.* He further bargained with the slave that he would free the slave when the slave paid him a certain sum of money. The situation seems unreal because the money is the slave's owner's in any event. But the realities are that the slave would be earning money outside of the household, the owner would allow him to retain for the *peculium* either a fixed proportion or any excess above a fixed amount, and the owner's aim would be to maximize his own benefit. The incentive of freedom would make the slave more industrious and obedient, and the owner would be profiting from the slave's earnings. From the money received from the slave for freedom, the owner could buy another and younger slave. In this text the slave gives his owner the sum agreed upon, but the owner then dies before he has freed the slave. It turns out that the owner had freed the slave in his will and had also left him a legacy of the *peculium*. The extent of the *peculium* has now to be established. In particular, the freedman wants to know whether the sum he had given the owner in return for a manumission that did not take place remains part of the *peculium* or not. The jurist's response is along purely formal lines. If the slave's owner had recorded it in his account books as being directly his own, the sum was removed from the *peculium;* if, on the other hand, he had recorded it as belonging to the slave it remained part of the *peculium*. There is no question of looking at the intention of the owner, of examining the realities of the situation, or of deciding upon the basis of fairness.

The parallels between fetial law and Roman private law deserve to be set out. The first stages in the run-up to the declaration of war have the form of a *legis actio*. The actual declaration corresponds to the *legis actio per manus iniectionem,* personal execution of judgment, with the hurling of the spear replacing the grasping by the hand. The warring parties called upon a god or gods to judge; the parties to a private lawsuit likewise chose the judge. The *pater patratus* was personally liable in the declaration of war for a fault on the part of his principal, the state, just as a *cognitor* was personally condemned in the action he brought on behalf of his principal. When a wrongdoer was surrendered to a foreign state, the wording used was that of noxal surrender in private law. Just as a father or owner was freed from further liability by the surrender of the son or slave, so the state was released from liability by the surrender of the wrongdoer. One should also note that the surrender of a city, which does not involve the fetials, has strong parallels with private law. The city must have been independent, *in sua potestate;* and there were two types of surrender, *in potestatem* and *in fidem,* the former corresponding to a standard private law transfer, the latter to a transfer in *fiducia*. Strikingly, the formalities here also have no imprint from religion. The parallels with private law are the more striking in that, according to Cicero, the most skilled interpreters of treaties and the most scrupulous in examining the relations between states are those who have commanded armies, and waged war, rather than even the most skilled jurists.[22]

Legalistic Roman religion and formalistic Roman secular law are two sides of the same coin. That, of course, does not explain why the Romans were the most religious people. But we are, perhaps, close to a plausible hypothesis.

The Romans were the most successful military nation in antiquity, and from an early date their economy was based on conquest and slavery. Given their legalism, it is not surprising that their declarations of war were in the form of a legal process. Given their religiosity, it cannot surprise that in this judgment the judges were the gods. And, given their practicality, for the Romans the judges had to render judgment before fighting began.

But then in these circumstances, it was vital that religiously the Romans do everything properly. The gods, as judges, cannot be (and were not) asked to play favorites. The Romans must, precisely, accurately, and formulaically, perform all the rituals and complete all the observances, to ensure a just war. For Roman religion, personal piety in the leaders was, of course, not a requirement. But every Roman victory in war confirmed the belief that their religious approach was correct and advantageous.

Thus, as long as the Romans wished to dominate in war, so long had they to be the most religious of peoples, at least until cynicism overwhelmed the state religion. They, themselves, were not slow to put together their religiosity and their worldly success.[23] In a revealing passage, after recounting disasters suffered by some leaders, Cicero continues:

> *De natura deorum*, 2.3.8. Caelius writes that Gaius Flaminius, after ignoring religion, fell at Trasimene, with a terrible blow to the state. From the fate of these men it can be understood that our state was increased by those leaders who obeyed the rules of religion. And if we

wish to compare our characteristics with foreigners, we are found to be in other matters equal or even inferior, yet in religion, that is in the cult of the gods, we are far superior.[24]

Elsewhere Cicero also relates:

*De harispicum responsis,* 9.19. . . . Or who once he is convinced that gods exist, is not also convinced that it is by their power that this great empire was born, and increased, and maintained?[25]

Such also was the belief among outsiders. We found it already in a passage quoted in chapter 1 from Dionysius of Halicarnassus, describing the fetial college: "It is incumbent on me to relate how many and how great affairs fall under its jurisdiction, to the end that those who are unacquainted with the piety practiced by the Romans of those times may not be surprised to find that all their wars had the most successful outcome."[26]

In a similar way, failure to observe the religious proprieties could be adjudged the prime reason for defeat in battle. One of the greatest Roman defeats in the Republic was that of the consul, C. Flaminius, by Hannibal at the battle of Lake Trasimene in 217 B.C., in which Flaminius was himself killed. Following upon this, Q. Fabius Maximus was appointed *dictator.* Livy records:

22.9.7. Quintus Fabius Maximus, dictator for the second time, on the very day he entered upon his office, convened the senate. Taking up first the issue of the gods, he persuaded the senators that the consul, C. Flaminius, had erred more through neglect of the ceremonies and the auspices than through rashness and ignorance. He asserted that the gods themselves should be consulted as to what would propitiate their anger, 8. and persuaded the senators to do what was rarely done except when dire prodigies had been announced, and order the *decemviri* to consult the Sybilline books. 9. When the *decemviri* had inspected the books of fate, they reported to the senators that a vow made to Mars on account of the war had not been properly performed, and must be performed afresh and on an ampler scale: 10. that great games must be vowed to Jupiter, and temples to Venus Erycina and Mens; that supplications and a *lectistenium* must be celebrated; and that a Sacred Spring must be vowed, if they prospered in battle and the state remained in the condition it had been in before hostilities began.[27]

Due performance of religious rituals was vital for the continuance of Roman success in war.

Long after the disappearance of any meaningful role for the fetials themselves, the gods played in other ways an important role in the Roman conduct of war. It must remain an open question whether the fetial system as a peace-preserving mechanism backfired once Rome expanded beyond central Italy. Because of the nature of the evidence in early times, we cannot tell to what extent the *ius fetiale* inhibited war. And though the Romans at the time of the actual declaration of war believed the gods had given the verdict in their favor, so also would the Latins who opposed them. But once the enemy was beyond central Italy and had no fetials, the Roman *ius fetiale* might even act as a disincentive to peace. The Romans would always have the verdict of the gods in their favor, that their war was just; and successes in war would strengthen their conviction in their piety, and righteousness in dealing with other peoples.

# Notes

*Introduction*

1. I do not propose to discuss the semantic problem of whether Roman international law is truly international law, but see Ziegler and the authorities he cites; "Völkerrecht," pp. 68ff.

2. Individual international judicial processes were widespread in the Hellenistic world: see the survey by A. J. Marshall, "The Survival and Development of International Jurisdiction in the Greek World under Roman Rule," in *Aufstieg und Niedergang der römischen Welt,* II.13, ed. H. Temporini (Berlin, 1980), pp. 6263ff. Particularly interesting are the instances of Greek cities asking the Roman senate to act as arbiter. For arbitration in the international sphere in the ancient world and later, see, e.g., A. Nussbaum, *A Concise History of the Law of Nations,* 2nd ed. (New York, 1954).

3. Surprisingly perhaps, there is also somewhat of a parallel in Aeschylus's *Agamemnon* where the Trojan War is portrayed as a lawsuit between the house of Priam and that of Agamemnon, with the gods acting as judges: lines 41, 534–35, 810ff.

4. For works relating primarily to a later period, see, e.g., J. W. Rich, *Declaring War in the Roman Republic* (Brussels, (1976); S. Albert, *Bellum Iustum* (Kallmünz, 1979); V. Ilari, *Guerra e diritto rel mondo antico* (Milan, 1980).

5. See now Watson, *The State, Law and Religion,* p. x. The mystery surrounding early Roman history and religion is great, and scholarly

controversy immense: see the bibliography in *Social Struggles in Archaic Rome,* ed. K. A. Raaflaub (Berkeley, 1986), pp. 379ff. My failure to discuss the accuracy of our sources for early Rome should not be viewed as a failure to grasp the importance of the matter. But I have nothing to say on the general issue, and nothing to add on the plausibility of what we are told about law. The accuracy of the sources must always be suspect; for the fetials, see Saulnier, "Rôle."

6. Dumézil, *Archaic Religion,* 1: 90.

7. For the subsequent understanding of the *ius fetiale,* see in general V. Ilari, *L' interpretazione storica del diritto di guerra romano fra tradizione romanistica e giusnaturalismo* (Milan, 1981).

## Chapter One. The Fetiales

1. The etymology of the word *fetialis* is obscure; cf. Ogilvie, *Livy,* p. 110. Among the ancients, Servius linked it with *foedus* (treaty): *In Vergilii Aeneidon libris* 1.62; 4.242; 10.14; Varro with *fides* (faith): *De lingua latina,* 5.86; Paul with *ferire* (to strike), p. 91. A. Weiss conjectures that the word is connected with the cult of Juppiter Feretrius, Jupiter the Striker, in C. Daremberg and E. Saglio, *Dictionnaire des antiquités grecques et romaines* (Paris, 1896), 2:1095. A. Ernout and A. Meillet trace it from the root *\*dhé,* which indicated 'a law' in Indo-Iranian: *Dictionnaire étymologique de la langue latine,* 4th ed. (Paris, 1967), p. 231. See also Dumézil, *Archaic Religion,* 1:91.

2. Tacitus, *Annales,* 3.64; cf. Cicero, *De legibus,* 2.8–9.21. For the *septemviri epulones,* see, e.g., H. H. Scullard, *Festivals and Ceremonies of the Roman Republic* (Ithaca, N.Y., 1981), pp. 186–87.

3. Cicero, *De officiis,* 1.11.36; Livy, 9.9.3; Arnobius, *Adversus nationes,* 2.67; *C.I.L.* $1^2$ p. 202 el. XLI.

4. Cf. Saulnier, "Rôle," p. 175.

5. See also Plutarch, *Camillus,* 18: quoted in chapter 5.

6. "Mortuo rege Pompilio Tullum Hostilium populus regem interrege rogante comitiis curiatis creavit, isque de imperio suo exemplo Pompilii populum consuluit curiatim. cuius excellens in re militari gloria magnaeque extiterunt res bellicae, fecitque idem et saepsit de manubiis comitium et curiam constituitque ius, quo bella indicerentur, quod per se iustissime inventum sanxit fetiali religione, ut omne bellum, quod denuntiatum indictumque non esset, id iniustum esse atque inpium iudicaretur."

7. *In Vergilii Aeneidon libris* 10.14.

8. *De viris illustribus,* 5.4.

9. "RES RAPUISSE LICEBIT clarigationem exercere, hoc est per fetiales bellum indicere: nam Ancus Marcius cum videret populum Romanum, arden-

tem amore bellorum, et plerumque inferre bella gentibus nulla iusta extante ratione, et exinde pericula creari, misit ad gentem Aequicula- nam et accepit ius fetiale, per quae bellum indicebatur hoc modo, sicut etiam de Albanis retulit Livius. Nam siquando homines vel animalia ab aliqua gente rapta essent populo Romano, cum fetialibus, id est sacerdotibus qui faciendis praesunt foederibus, profiscebatur etiam pater patratus et ante fines stans clara voce dicebat belli causam, et nolentibus res raptas restituere vel auctores iniuriae tradere, iaciebat hastam, quae res erat pugnae principium, et iam sic licebat more belli res rapere. Clarigatio autem dicta est aut a clara voce, qua utebatur pater patratus aut a ξλήρῳ hoc est sorte: nam per bellicam sortem invadebant agros hostium: unde et ξληρονόμοι dicuntur graece qui iure sortiuntur bona defuncti."

10. "Ut tamen, quoniam Numa in pace religiones instituisset, a se bellicae caerimoniae proderentur, nec gererentur solum sed etiam indice- rentur bella aliquo ritu, ius ab antiqua gente Aequicolis, quod nunc fetiales habent, descripsit quo res repetuntur." But Livy also has a different version. He represents fetials at operation in 1.24 under King Tullus and fetials may also be envisaged at 1.22: cf., e.g., R. J. Penella, "War, Peace, and the *ius fetiale* in Livy 1," *Classical Philology* 82 (1987): 233ff.

11. Livy, 1.32.11; cf., e.g., Ogilvie, *Livy,* p. 127.

12. Dionysius of Halicarnassus, 2.72; Servius, *In Vergilii Aeneidon libris* 10.14.

13. See Dessau in *C.I.L.* 14, p. 187, n. 2.

14. Livy, 1.24.4.

15. *In Vergilii Aeneidon libris* 7.695.

16. See, e.g., E. T. Salmon, *The Making of Roman Italy* (Ithaca, N.Y., 1982), p. 26.

17. ". . . iustos autem dicit Faliscos, quia populus Romanus missis decem viris ab ipsis iura fetialia et non nulla supplementa duodecim tabu- larum accepit, quas habuerat ab Atheniensibus."

18. Cf., e.g., Wieacker, *Rechtsgeschichte,* 1: 287ff., and the authors he cites.

19. *C.I.L.* 6.1302; Iulius Paris's epitome of an unknown author's *Liber de praenominibus*—to be found in C. Kempf's edition of Valerius Max- imus, 2nd ed. (Stuttgart, 1966), p. 588. (This is an *elogium:* A. Degrassi, *Inscriptiones Italiae XIII: fasc. III: Elogia* [Rome, 1937], pp. 42–43, no. 66); Aurelius Victor, *De viris illustribus,* 5.4; Dionysius of Halicarnassus, 2.72.

20. Cf., e.g., G. Radke in *Der Kleine Pauly,* vol. 1 (Stuttgart, 1964), p. 96.

21. Dionysius of Halicarnassus, 2.72.

22. The suggestion of Catalano, *Linee,* 1:21, that the *ius fetiale* was com-

mon to the people of the *koiné* Etrusco-Italian is not supported by the evidence.

23. See Ziegler, "Völkerrecht," pp. 72ff., and the authors he cites.

24. A different, and unacceptable explanation is found in Servius, *In Vergilii Aeneidon libris* 8.641. The suggestion is that the stone was substituted by the fetials for the swords previously used because they considered the flint stone to be a symbol of ancient Jupiter. This explanation is obviously anachronistic.

25. See, e.g., Samter, "Feriae Latinae," in *RE* 6, cols. 2213ff.; "Juppiter Latiaris," in *RE* 10, cols. 1134–35. Latte, *Religionsgeschichte*, pp. 144ff.; cf., e.g., A. Alföldi, *Early Rome and the Latins* (Ann Arbor, Mich., n.d.), pp. 19ff.

26. Dionysius of Halicarnassus, 4.49; Macrobius, *Saturnalia*, 1.16.16.

27. The term *collegium fetialium* occurs in Livy, 36.3.7.

28. Nonius, quoting from book 2 of Varro, *De vita populi Romani*, p. 850.

29. Dionysius of Halicarnassus, 2.72.

30. Livy, 8.38.1.

31. Livy, 8.17.5.

32. See, e.g., *C.I.L.* 6.913, 1497; 8.6987;

33. *Res gestae divi Augusti*, 7.

34. Suetonius, *Claudius*, 25.

35. Cassius Dio, 72.33.3. For a list of the fetials in the early Empire, see M. W. Hoffman Lewis, *The Official Priests of Rome under the Julio-Claudians* (Rome, 1955).

36. Except in Gallic wars: Plutarch, *Camillus*, 41.6.

37. "Foedera alia aliis legibus, ceterum eodem modo omnia fiunt. Tum ita factum accepimus, nec ullius vetustior foederis memoria est. Fetialis regem Tullum ita rogavit: 'Iubesne me, rex, cum patre patrato populi Albani foedus ferire?' Iubente rege 'Sagmina,' inquit, 'te, rex, posco.' Rex aid: Puram tollito.' Fetialis ex arce graminis herbam puram attulit. Postea regem ita rogavit: 'Rex, facisne me tu regium nuntium populi Romani Quiritium, vasa comitesque meos?' Rex respondit: 'Quod sine fraude mea populique Romani Quiritium fiat, facio.' Fetialis erat M. Valerius; is patrem patratum Sp. Fusium fecit verbena caput capillosque tangens. Pater patratus ad ius iurandum patrandum, id est sanciendum fit foedus; multisque id verbis, quae longo effata carmine non operae est referre, peragit."

38. *In Vergilli Aeneidon libris* 12.120.

39. *Naturalis historia*, 2.3.5; see also Festus, s.v. *sagmina;* Livy, 30.43.9; D.1.8.8.1; Ogilvie, *Livy*, p. 111.

40. Varro, in Nonius, 528.

41. See also Varro, in Nonius, 529.

42. See, e.g., Wissowa, *Religion und Kultus*, p. 118.

43. Servius, *In Vergilii Aeneidon libris* 12.206: Paul, p. 92. For ceremonies using the flint stone, see chapter 3.
44. Pluturch confuses *pater patratus* with *pater patrimus; Quaestiones Romanae,* 62; cf. Festus, s.v. *pater patrimus.* See also Cicero, *De oratore,* 1.40.181; *Pro Caecina,* 34.98. Cf. Ernout and Meillet, *Dictionnaire étymologique,* pp. 488–89.
45. Servius, *In Vergilii Aeneidon libris* 12.206. Elsewhere in the same work, at 8.641, it is said that the ancients took the flint stone as the symbol of Jupiter.
46. Dionysius of Halicarnassus, 2.72.6.
47. Servius, *In Vergilii Aeneidon libris* 12.120.
48. Livy, 1.32.6.
49. Oddly some texts make it appear that in some circumstances four fetials proceeded to the boundaries: Varro, in Nonius, 529; Livy, 1.24.5; 30.43.9. The point need not detain us but see Samter, "Fetiales," in *RE* 6, cols. 2259ff.; Wissowa, *Religion und Kultus,* p. 551 and n. 5.

*Chapter Two.* Testis, Witness: Testis, *Judge*

1. See, e.g., M. Kaser, *Das altrömische Ius* (Göttingen, 1949), pp. 20ff.; G. Donatuti, "La *clarigatio* o *rerum repititio* e l'istituto parallelo dell' antica procedura civile romana," *IURA* 6 (1955): 31ff.; E. Volterra, "L'instituto della *clarigatio* e l'antica procedura delle *legis actiones,*" *Scritti Carnelutti* 4 (Padua, 1950): 243ff.; H. Hausmaninger, " 'Bellum iustum' und 'iusta causa belli' im älteren römischen Recht," "*Österreichische Zeitschrift für öffentliches Recht*" (1961): 340; Ogilvie, *Livy,* p. 127; Ziegler, "Völkerrecht," p. 103.
2. This is the translation of B. O. Foster in the Loeb Classical Library, *Livy* (Cambridge, Mass., 1967), 1:117. " 'Audi, Iuppiter, et tu, Iane Quirine, dique omnes caelestes vosque, terrestres, vosque, inferni, audite. Ego vos testor populum illum'—quicumque est nominat—'iniustum esse neque ius persolvere. Sed de istis rebus in patria maiores natu consulemus quo pacto ius nostrum adipiscamur.' "
3. See, e.g., Wissowa, *Religion und Kultus,* pp. 550, 552; Dumézil, *Archaic Religion,* 1:273 (dealing with Livy, 1.24.7–8); 2:590.
4. Kaser, *Das altrömische Ius* (Göttingen, 1949), p. 21.
5. But there is nothing strange in calling the gods to be witnesses: see, e.g., Homer, *Odyssey,* 1.273; 2.211.
6. The exact path of development is disputed, but there are no doubts that the descent of *testis* is from a meaning of 'third person'. See, e.g., A. Ernout and A. Meillet, *Dictionnaire étymologique de la lanque latine,* 4th ed. (Paris, 1967), p. 689; A. Walde and J. B. Hofmann, *Lateinisches*

*etymologisches Wörterbuch,* 5th ed. (Heidelberg, 1982), 2:676–77; *Oxford Latin Dictionary* (Oxford, 1982), p. 1932.

7. "Legatus ubi ad fines eorum venit unde res repetuntur, capite velato filo—lanae velamen est—'Audi, Iuppiter,' inquit; 'audite, fines'— cuiuscumque gentis sunt nominat;—'audiat fas. Ego sum publicus nuntius populi Romani; iuste pieque legatus venio verbisque meis fides sit.' Peragit deinde postulata. 7. Inde Iovem testem facit: 'Si ego iniuste impieque illos homines illasque res dedier mihi exposco, tum patriae compotem me numquam siris esse.' "

8. See, e.g., Ernout and Meillet, *Dictionnaire,* p. 195; E. Benveniste, *Le vocabulaire des institutions indo-européennes* (Paris, 1969), 1:137; A. Watson, *"Emptio,* 'taking'," *Glotta* 53 (1975): 294ff.

9. In an equivalent context, Plutarch gives as the Greek equivalent of *testare* 'to witness' the word μαρτυράμενοι and this certainly means 'witnesses': *Numa,* 12.4. See also Dionysius of Halicarnassus, 2.72.6. But that had come to be the standard meaning of *testis* and *testari* long before Plutarch and Dionysius. The passages only mean that Plutarch and Dionysius no longer understood the original meaning of the form.

10. "Ad haec Tullus 'Nuntiate,' inquit, 'regi vestro regem Romanum deos facere testes uter prius populus res repetentes legatos aspernatus dimiserit, ut in eum omnes expetant huiusce clades belli.' "

11. See, e.g., Thomas, *Textbook,* p. 104.

12. See, e.g., Kaser, *Zivilprozessrecht,* pp. 47ff.

13. See, e.g., Thomas, *Textbook,* pp. 75ff.; Kaser suggests that originally the magistrate would have chosen the judge, but from a very early date he would have listened to the parties' wishes, especially to reject a judge, and the parties' right to choose developed from this: *Zivilprozessrecht,* p. 43. There is no evidence for this proposition. That the magistrate officially appoints does not imply that he had the right to choose.

14. Kaser, *Zivilprozessrecht,* p. 57.

15. For this meaning for *ordinato iudicio,* see Kaser, *Zivilprozessrecht,* p. 57, n. 34.

16. "Contestari litem dicuntur duo aut plures adversarii, quod ordinato iudicio—utraque pars dicere solet: testes estote."

17. "Contestari est, cum uterque reus dicit: testes estote." For *reus* meaning party to a lawsuit see Festus, s.v. *reus.*

In these two passages s.v. *contestari,* Festus uses the present tense, which is unusual for him when describing something no longer in use. On that account M. Wlassak attributes *testes estote* to the formulary procedure, since *legis actiones* were obsolete: *Die Litiskontestation im Formularprozess* (Leipzig, 1899), pp. 69ff. This view has found little support: see, e.g., G. Jahr, *Litis Contestatio* (Cologne, 1960), pp. 21–22. Against it I would also urge that there is no place in the formulary system for using such words with a formal impact.

18. See, e.g., Wlassak, *Litiskontestation,* p. 81; Jahr, *Litis Contestatio,* p. 21.

19. This is so whether witnesses were called to testify to the facts on which the case is based, or to note the proceedings.

 I believe that it is because the calling on witnesses is too unimportant to be the decisive moment for *litis contestatio* that Wlassak and others take this role from *testes estote* and relate it to the whole declaration: *Litiskontestation,* p. 81; cf. E. Weiss, in *RE* 13, col. 777; Jahr, *Litis Contestatio,* pp. 59ff. But against such a view is the very term *litis contestatio,* which refers to a calling on *testes:* cf. Kaser, *Zivilprozessrecht,* pp. 57ff. And there is the express testimony of Festus.

20. G.4.15. Subsequently, by the *lex Pinaria* the judge was appointed only after thirty days.

21. See, e.g., Kaser, *Zivilprozessrecht,* pp. 61–62; Wieacker, *Rechtsgeschichte,* 1:273.

22. G.4.13.

23. See, e.g., V. Arangio-Ruiz, *Cours de droit romain (les actions)* (Naples, 1935), p. 13, who takes the words as a call to the assembled citizens to remember exactly what happened.

24. G.4.15.

25. See, e.g., G. Rotondi, *Leges publicae populi romani* (Milan, 1912), pp. 472–73.

26. G.4.17a.

27. See, e.g., Kaser, *Zivilprozessrecht,* p. 23 and n. 42; Wieacker, *Rechtsgeschichte,* 1:223; R. Yaron, "Semitic Elements in Early Rome," in *Daube Noster,* ed. A. Watson (Edinburgh, 1974), pp. 351ff.; C. W. Keyes, *Cicero, de re publica, de legibus* (Cambridge, Mass., 1966), p. 466, n. 1; A. Momigliano, "Praetor maximus e questione affini," in *Studi in onore di Giuseppe Grosso* (Turin, 1968), 1:161ff.

28. Dumézil, *Archaic Religion,* 1:110.

29. "In Commentariis Consularibus scriptum sic inveni: Qui exercitum imperaturus erit, accenso dicito: 'C. Calpurni, voca inlicium omnes Quirites huc ad me.' Accensus dicit sic: 'Omnes Quirites, inlicium vos ite huc ad iudices.' 'C. Calpurni,' cos. dicit, 'voca ad conventionem omnes Quirites huc ad me.' Accensus dicit sic: 'Omnes Quirites, ite ad conventionem huc ad iudices.' Dein consul eloquitur ad exercitum: 'Impero qua convenit ad comitia centuriata.' "

30. See, e.g., Keyes, *Cicero,* p. 466, n.1.

31. For the correct approach, see already Yaron, "Semitic Elements," pp. 351–52.

32. See, e.g., Wieacker, *Rechtsgeschichte,* 1:233, n.10.

33. S.v. *meddix.*
34. See, e.g., T. Mommsen, *Römisches Staatsrecht,* 3rd ed. (Leipzig, 1887), 2:74ff.
35. See *Tab.* 2.1b; 2.2; 9.3.
36. "Familiam pecuniamque tuam endo mandatela tua custodelaque mea esse aio, eaque, quo tu iure testamentum facere possis secundum legem publicam hoc aere aenaeque libra esto mihi empta."
37. For the *testamentum per aes et libram,* see A. Watson, *Rome of the XII Tables* (Princeton, 1975), pp. 52ff.
38. "Haec, ita ut in his tabulis cerisque scripta sunt, ita do, ita lego, ita testor, itaque vos quirites testimonium mihi perhibetote" (*G*.2.104).
39. No argument contrary to the thesis propounded here can be drawn from the etymology of the word *testamentum.* That word must be later than *testis* from which it derives, and it may easily date from a time when the principal meaning of *testis* was 'witness'. Again, the original true will was made in the *comitia calata* and, because of the sparseness of the evidence, we cannot tell whether the populace so assembled was simply to act as witnesses or, as in the case of *adrogatio,* to approve the will by a legislative act: cf. Watson, *Rome of the XII Tables,* p. 65. In the latter alternative, an original sense for *testamentum* akin to 'an act of judging' would be appropriate.
40. Nörr, *Aspekte,* p. 13. Kaser also sees the just war as a trial process without a judge appointed from above: *Zivilprozessrecht,* p. 18.
41. See A. Watson, *The Nature of Law* (Edinburgh, 1977), pp. 1ff.

*Chapter Three. Declarations of War*

1. That the envoy was a fetial emerges from Livy, 1.32.5. Dionysius of Halicarnassus, 2.72.6, says the fetial was chosen by his colleagues.
2. Servius, *In Verg. Aen.* 9.52; Livy, 8.14.6; Arnobius, *Adversus nationes,* 2.67.
3. The Latin text is quoted in chapter 2, n. 7.
4. *G*.4.17a; cf. Ogilvie, *Livy,* p. 127. Also see Ogilvie, *Livy,* p. 130, for the threefold invocation. I follow Dumézil, *Archaic Religion,* 1:91 (against K. Latte, "Religiöse Begriffe in frührömishen Recht," *Zeitschrift der Savigny Stiftung (romanistische Abteilung)* 67 [1950]: 56, and Ogilvie, *Livy,* p. 132) that an early Roman personification of *fas* is perfectly possible.
5. See, e.g., the texts in *D*.49.15.
6. See, e.g., *D*.49.15.2; 49.15.3; 11.7.36.
7. The statement is not an oath since the fetial does not swear his veracity by a god; but he has called upon Jupiter to act as judge.
8. *G*.4.13, 14.

9. "Nunc admonendi sumus agere nos aut nostro nomine aut alieno, veluti cognitorio, procuratorio, tutorio, curatorio, cum olim, quo tempore legis actiones in usu fuissent, alieno nomine agere non liceret, praeterquam ex certis causis."

10. "Nunc admonendi sumus, agere posse quemlibet aut suo nomine aut alieno. alieno veluti procuratorio, tutorio, curatorio, cum olim in usu fuisset, alterius nomine agere non posse nisi pro populo, pro libertate, pro tutela. praeterea lege Hostilia permissum est furti agere eorum nomine qui apud hostes essent aut rei publicae causa abessent quive in eorum cuius tutela essent. et quia hoc non minimam incommoditatem habebat, quod alieno nomine neque agere neque excipere actionem licebat, coeperunt homines per procuratores litigare: nam et morbus et aetas et necessaria peregrinatio itemque aliae multae causae saepe impedimento sunt quo minus rem suam ipsi exsequi possint."

11. See, e.g., F. de Zulueta, *The Institutes of Gaius* (Oxford, 1953), 2:274.

12. J. A. C. Thomas, *The Institutes of Justinian* (Cape Town, 1975), p. 309.

13. Kaser, *Zivilprozessrecht,* p. 46 and n. 27.

14. He refers to Festus, s.v. *vindiciae:* Kaser, *Zivilprozessrecht,* p. 46 and n. 24.

15. "Qui autem alieno nomine agit, intentionem quidem ex persona domini sumit, condemnationem autem in suam personam convertit . . ."

16. See, e.g., Livy, 39.25.10; Tacitus, *Historiae,* 3.80; Seneca, *De ira,* 3.2.5; Nepos, *Pelopidas,* 5.1; *D*.48.6.7; 50.7.18(17).

17. Livy, 1.32.8; see also Dionysius of Halicarnassus, 2.72.7, which is quoted in chapter 1.

18. *G*.4.17b. "Quando tu negas, in diem tricensimum tibi iudicis capiendi causa condico."

19. The Latin is quoted in chapter 2, n. 2.

20. "Tum nuntius Romam ad consulendum redit. Confestim rex his ferme verbis patres consulebat: 11. 'Quarum rerum, litium, causarum condixit pater patratus populi Romani Quiritium patri patrato Priscorum Latinorum hominibusque Priscis Latinis, quas res nec dederunt nec solverunt nec fecerunt, quas res dari, solvi, fieri oportuit, dic,' inquit ei quem primum sententiam rogabat, 'quid censes?' 12. Tum ille: 'Puro pioque duello quaerendas censeo itaque consentio consciscoque.' Inde ordine alii rogabantur; quandoque pars maior eorum qui aderant in eandem sententiam ibat, bellum erat consensum."

21. See, e.g., Ogilvie, *Livy,* p. 133.

22. See, above all, D. Daube, *Forms of Roman Legislation* (Oxford, 1956), pp. 8ff.; cf. A. Watson, *The Law of Obligations in the Later Roman Republic* (Oxford, 1965), p. 87 and n. 5.

23. With Ogilvie, *Livy,* p. 135, I prefer to take the adjective *sanguineus* as referring to cornel, rather than meaning 'bloodstained'.
24. For the magical qualities of iron, see Ogilvie, *Livy,* p. 135.
25. "Fieri solitum ut fetialis hastam ferratam aut praeustam sanguineam ad fines eorum ferret et non minus tribus puberibus praesentibus diceret: 13. 'Quod populi Priscorum Latinorum hominesque Prisci Latini adversus populum Romanum Quiritium fecerunt, deliquerunt, quod populus Romanus Quiritium bellum cum Priscis Latinis iussit esse senatusque populi Romani Quiritium censuit, consensit, conscivit, ut bellum cum Priscis Latinis fieret, ob eam rem ego populusque Romanus populis Priscorum Latinorum hominibusque Priscis Latinis bellum indico facioque.' id ubi dixisset, hastam in fines eorum emittebat. 14. Hoc tum modo ab Latinis repetitae res ac bellum indictum, moremque eum posteri acceperunt."

    See also the rather uninformative passage in Aulus Gellius, *Noctes Atticae,* 16.4.1. The Hermunduli are otherwise unknown.
26. "Per manus iniectionem aeque ⟨de⟩ his rebus agebatur, de quibus ut ita ageretur lege aliqua cautum est, veluti iudicati lege XII tabularum. quae actio talis erat: qui agebat sic dicebat: QUOD TU MIHI IUDICATUS (sive DAMNATUS) ES SESTERTIUM X MILIA, QUANDOC NON SOLVISTI, OB EAM REM EGO TIBI SESTERTIUM X MILIUS IUDICATI MANUM INICO; et simul aliquam partem corporis eius prendebat. nec licebat iudicato manum sibi depellere et pro se lege agere, sed vindicem dabat, qui pro se causam agere solebat. qui vindicem non dabat, domum ducebatur ab actore et uinciebatur."
27. We would have been told of them, just as we are for the various formulations *in iure.*
28. See already, Dumézil, *Archaic Religion,* 1:208, who, however, persists in seeing the gods called to witness.
29. Polybius, 3.25.6, describing the oath in the treaty of 279 B.C., says that the Romans following an old custom swore by Mars and Quirinus. It is important that this is not a declaration of war, but a treaty, which is not cast in the form of a court action.
30. Dionysius of Halicarnassus, 2.72.6ff.; Plutarch, *Numa,* 12.4–5; Cicero, *De re publica,* 2.17; Livy, 1.32.
31. "FAETIALES apud veteres Romanos erant, qui sancto legatorum officio ab his, qui adversum populum Romanum vi aut rapinis aut iniuriis hostili mente conmoverant, pignera facto foedere iure repetebant; nec bella indicebantur, quae tamen pia vocabant, priusquam quid fuisset faetialibus denuntiatum. Varro de Vita Populi Romani lib. II: 'itaque bella et tarde et magna diligentia suscipiebant, quod bellum nullum nisi pium putabant geri oportere: priusquam indicerent bellum is, a

quibus iniurias factas sciebant, faetiales legatos res repetitum mittebant quattuor, quos oratores vocabant.' "

32. *De re publica,* 2.17.31; 3.23.35; *De officiis,* 1.11.36.

33. Livy, 1.32.7, 11, 13; See also Cicero, *De re publica,* 3.23.35; Dionysius of Halicarnassus, 2.72.5ff.; Plutarch, *Numa* 12.4–5; Isidorus, *Etymologiae,* 18.1.2ff.

34. "Irae adversus Veientes in insequentem annum, C. Servilium Ahalam L. Papirium Mugillanum consules, dilatae sunt. 13. Tunc quoque ne confestim bellum indiceretur neve exercitus mitterentur religio obstitit; fetiales prius mittendos ad res repetendas censuere. 14. Cum Veientibus nuper acie dimicatum ad Nomentum et Fidenas fuerat, indutiaeque inde, non pax facta, quarum et dies exierat et ante diem rebellaverant; missi tamen fetiales; nec eorum, cum more patrum iurati repeterent res, verba sunt audita. 15. Controversia inde fuit utrum populi iussu indiceretur bellum an satis esset senatus consultum. Pervicere tribuni, denuntiando impedituros se dilectum, ut Quinctius consul de bello ad populum ferret. 16. Omnes centuriae iussere. In eo quoque plebs superior fuit, quod tenuit ne consules in proximum annum crearentur."

35. Livy, 1.32; Dionysius of Halicarnassus, 2.72.8–9.

36. Plutarch, *Numa,* 12.6; Livy, 38.45.4ff. But the point is best brought out by the Roman insistence on discovering whether Hannibal had waged war without proper Carthaginian authorization.

37. The suggestion of Catalano, *Linee,* 1:29, that the *ius fetiale* was common to all peoples is not supported by the evidence.

38. "Illa iniusta bella sunt, quae sunt sine causa suscepta. nam extra ulciscendi aut propulsandorum hostium causam bellum geri iustum nullum potest . . ." (Isidorus, *Orig.* 18.1).

39. "Nullum bellum iustum nisi denuntiatum, nisi indictum, nisi repetitis rebus."

40. See also A. J. Holloday and M. D. Goodman, "Religious Scruples in Ancient Warfare," *Classical Quarterly* 36 (1986): 160ff.

*Chapter Four. Treaty Making*

1. "Pater patratus ad ius iurandum patrandum, id est sanciendum fit foedus; multisque id verbis, quae longo effata carmine non operae est referre, peragit" (Livy, 1.24.6).

2. "Legibus deinde recitatis 'Audi,' inquit, 'Iuppiter, audi, pater patrate populi Albani, audi tu, populus Albanus. Ut illa palam prima postrema ex illis tabulis cerave recitata sunt sine dolo malo utique ea hic hodie rectissime intellecta sunt, illis legibus populus Romanus prior non deficiet.' "

3. In the promise of dowry by *dotis dictio,* only the promisor speaks, but there are special reasons for that: cf. A. Watson, *The Law of Persons in the Later Roman Republic* (Oxford, 1967), pp. 57ff.

4. But one should make nothing of the fact that the *pater patratus* is the agent of the Roman people and binds them, though there was no agent in Roman contract law. An entity such as a people has to act through a representative.

5. In this book I stress the parallels between the fetial law and private law. But in contract law, the early *stipulatio* determined the evolution of other contracts to the virtual exclusion of other sources of influence: see A. Watson, *Roman Law and Comparative Law* (Athens, Ga., 1991), pp. 122ff. Thus, no bilateral oral contract developed—nor did private law contracts that required the presence of witnesses or of writing, yet such contracts are documented for Rome's first treaty with Carthage, reputably of 509 B.C.: Polybius, 3.22.2. On this clause of the treaty, see, e.g., M. David, "The Treaties between Rome and Carthage," in *Symbolae ad Jus et Historiam pertinentes Julio Christiano Van Oven dedicatae,* ed. M. David, B. A. van Groningen, and E. M. Meijers (Leiden, 1946), pp. 235–36.

   On the treaties between Rome and Carthage, see in general H. Bengtson, *Die Verträge der griechisch-römischen Welt* (Munich, 1962), 2:16ff.; on the *foedus Cassianum* giving equal rights to Romans and Latins, his *Verträge,* 2:22ff. He conveniently collects the sources. Paradisi shrewdly observes that the *foedus Cassianum* seems to translate ancient customs among the peoples of the *nomen Latinum* into clauses of agreement. He hypothesizes that the clauses may rest on earlier examples: "Due aspetti," p. 207.

6. *C.I.L.* 6.2059.

7. Dumézil, *Archaic Religion,* 1:92.

8. Dumézil's other suggestion is that *tabulae* refers to bare tablets of metal or stone on which the treaty was engraved, and *cera* to wooden tablets coated with wax in which the treaty was incised.

9. For some scholars, notably Ogilvie, *Livy,* p. 111, *tabulis cerave* is an anachronism borrowed from the later form of the will *per aes et libram,* but see the arguments in Dumézil. For a parallel precautionary phrase in augural formulas see now J. Linderski, "The Augural Law," in *Aufstieg und Niedergang der römischen Welt,* II.16.3, ed. H. Temporini (Berlin, 1986), p. 2269.

10. " 'Si prior defexit publico consilio dolo malo, tum tu ille Diespiter populum Romanum sic ferito ut ego hunc porcum hic hodie feriam; tantoque magis ferito quanto magis potes pollesque.' 9. Id ubi dixit, porcum saxo silice percussit. Sua item carmina Albani suumque ius iurandum per suum dictatorem suosque sacerdotes peregerunt."

11. "Semitic Influences in Early Rome," in *Daube Noster,* ed. A. Watson (Edinburgh, 1974), pp. 343ff.

12. Polybius, 3.22, concerns the first Roman treaty with Carthage, and, as Yaron rightly states, gives only the substantive provisions. Polybius, 7.9, concerns the treaty of Hannibal and Philip of Macedon. It is made "in the presence of" gods including the "gods of the army who preside over this oath." But the gods are not said to be guarantors of the oath. On the treaty, see M. L. Barré, *The God-list in the Treaty between Hannibal and Philip V of Macedonia* (Baltimore, 1983).

13. " . . . vel a porca foede, hoc est, lapidibus caesa, . . . " (In Vergilii Aeneidon libris, 1.62; cf. the same work, 8.641).

    The sacrifice of the pig by the fetials is shown for the making of a treaty, specifically with the Gabini—a document attesting the early treaty between Rome and Gabii was apparently found in Augustus's time—in Roman coins of around 15 B.C.: H. A. Grueber, *Coins of the Roman Republic in the British Museum* (London, 1910), 2:56, 98, nos. 4492, 4493, 4660.

14. Polybius, 3.22ff. The dating is controverted, but the exact date is not critical here: but see, e.g., F. W. Walbank, *A Historical Commentary on Polybius* (Oxford, 1957), 1:337–38.

15. "Fetiales cum in Africam ad foedus feriundum ire iuberentur, ipsis postulantibus senatus consultum in haec verba factum est, ut privos lapides silices privasque verbenas secum ferrent, ut, ubi praetor Romanus iis imperaret ut foedus ferirent, illi praetorem sagmina poscerent. Herbae id genus ex arce sumptum fetialibus dari solet."

16. But we have no need here to go into the question of any possible differences between a *foedus aequum* and a *foedus iniquum;* and between *hospitium* and *amicitia:* see, however, Ziegler and the authorities he cites, "Völkerrecht," pp. 82ff.

17. "Consules profecti ad Pontium in conloquium, cum de foedere victor agitaret, negarunt iniussu populi foedus fieri posse nec sine fetialibus caerimoniaque alia sollemni. 2. Itaque non, ut uolgo credunt Claudiusque etiam scribit, foedere pax Caudina sed per sponsionem facta est. 3. Quid enim aut sponsoribus in foedere opus esset aut obsidibus, ubi precatione res transigitur, per quem populum fiat quo minus legibus dictis stetur, ut eum ita Iuppiter feriat quemadmodum a fetialibus porcus feriatur?"

18. See, e.g., Ziegler, "Völkerrecht," pp. 93ff.

19. "Quae sententia testis erit mihine an legionibus vestris pepercerim, cum me seu turpi seu necessaria sponsione, obstrinxi; 5. qua tamen, quando iniussu populi facta est, non tenetur populus Romanus, nec quicquam ex ea praeterquam corpora nostra debentur Samnitibus. 6. Dedamur per fetiales nudi vinctique; exsolvamus religione populum,

si qua obligavimus, ne quid divini humanive obstet quo minus iustum piumque de integro ineatur bellum."

20. "Tum ubi in coetum Samnitium et ad tribunal ventum Ponti est, A. Cornelius Arvina fetialis ita verba fecit. 'Quandoque hisce homines iniussu populi Romani Quiritium foedus ictum iri spoponderunt atque ob eam rem noxam nocuerunt, ob eam rem quo populus Romanus scelere impio sit solutus hosce homines vobis dedo.' "

21. Ziegler, "Völkerrecht," pp. 93–94. For an illuminating discussion of earlier interpretations of the text, see F. La Rosa, "Sulla 'sponsio' delle Forche caudine," *IURA* 1 (1950); 283ff.

22. To evade the difficulty, the *stipulatio* was framed conditionally: "Do you promise to pay 200 if X does not pay 100?" But here we can be sure Postumius did not promise to surrender himself if the Romans did not perform his *sponsio*.

23. See, e.g., A. Watson, *The Law of Obligations in the Later Roman Republic* (Oxford, 1965), p. 274.

24. *D*.9.3.1.8; 9.4.2.1; 9.4.4*pr*; 30.45.1; 35.2.63*pr*.

25. See, e.g., W. W. Buckland, *Textbook of Roman Law*, 3rd ed., ed P. Stein (Cambridge, 1963), p. 603; Thomas, *Textbook*, p. 381.

*Chapter Five. Cautelary Jurisprudence and Judgments*

1. Dionysius of Halicarnassus, 2.72.5; Livy, 1.32.7.

2. "Consul deinde M'. Acilius ex senatus consulto ad collegium fetialium rettulit, ipsine utique regi Antiocho indiceretur bellum, an satis esset ad praesidium aliquod eius nuntiari, 8. et num Aetolis quoque separatim indici iuberent bellum, et num prius societas et amicitia eis renuntianda esset quam bellum indicendum. 9. Fetiales responderunt iam ante sese, cum de Philippo consulerentur, decrevisse nihil referre, ipsi coram an ad praesidium nuntiaretur; 10. amicitiam renuntiatam videri, cum legatis totiens repetentibus res nec reddi nec satisfieri aequum censuissent; 11. Aetolos ultro sibi bellum indixisse, cum Demetriadem, sociorum urbem, per vim occupassent, Chalcidem terra marique oppugnatum issent, 12. regem Antiochum in Europam ad bellum populo Romano inferendum traduxissent."

3. Varro, in Nonius, 529. It was the prerogative of the college to give advice, and the responsibility of individuals to recite formulas. For this distinction with regard to the augurs, see J. Linderski, "The Augural Law," in *Aufstieg und Niedergang der römischen Welt*, II.16.3, ed. H. Temporini (Berlin, 1986), p. 2151.

4. Livy, 31.8.3.

5. Livy, 38.42.7.

6. "Adversus eosdem hostes parem fidem in iure legationis tuendo patres

conscripti exhibuere: M. enim Aemilio Lepido, L. Flaminio consulibus L. Minucium et L. Manlium Karthaginiensium legatis, quia manus his attulerant, per fetiales a M. Claudio praetore dedendos curaverunt. se tunc senatus, non eos, quibus hoc praestabatur, aspexit." On the incident, see also Livy, 38.42.7.

7. Valerius Maximus, 6.6.5; Livy, *Periochae,* 15; Cassius Dio, 10fr.42; Zonaras, 8.7; cf. T. R. S. Broughton, "Mistreatment of Foreign Legates and the Fetial Priests: Three Roman Cases," *Phoenix* 41 (1987): 51.

It seems not possible to decide the procedure, and whether *fetiales* were involved, in the trial of L. Appuleius Saturninus around 102 or 101 b.c.: Diodorus Siculus, 36.15. But see Broughton, "Mistreatment," pp. 54ff.

8. See also, Cicero, *De officiis,* 3.30.109. Other texts also show action being taken, without the intervention of the fetials for breaches of international law; e.g., Livy, 6.1.6 (where a Roman ambassador had taken up arms against the Gauls: cf. Livy, 5.36.6); Cicero, *De oratore,* 1.40.181 (surrender of Roman who concluded an unpopular treaty: cf. 2.32.137ff.).

9. Though doubt is expressed by Samter, *"Fetiales,"* in *RE* 6, col. 2260.

10. "idem lib. III: 'si cuius legati violati essent, qui id fecissent, quamvis nobiles essent, uti dederentur civitati statuerunt; faetialesque viginti, qui de his rebus cognoscerent, iudicarent et statuerent et constituerent.' "

11. *Numa,* 12.3–7.

12. "Si quis legatum hostium pulsasset, contra ius gentium id commissum esse existimatur, quia sancti habentur legati. et ideo si, cum legati apud nos essent gentis alicuius, bellum cum eis indictum sit, responsum est liberos eos manere: id enim iuri gentium convenit esse. itaque cum, qui legatum pulsasset, Quintus Mucius dedi hostibus, quorum erant legati, solitus est respondere. quem hostes si non recepissent, quaesitum est, an civis Romanus maneret: quibusdam existimantibus manere, aliis contra, quia quem semel populus iussisset dedi, ex civitate expulsisse videretur, sicut faceret, cum aqua et igni interdiceret. in qua sententia videtur Publius Mucius fuisse. id autem maxime quaesitum est in Hostilio Mancino, quem Numantini sibi deditum non acceperunt: de quo tamen lex postea lata est, ut esset civis Romanus, et praeturam quoque gessisse dicitur."

Interestingly, this text seems to be the only one where a jurist might be using the words *ius gentium* to mean 'international law', though that usage is common among nonjurists: e.g., Livy, 5.36.6, 8; 6.1.6; Nepos, *Pelopidas,* 5.1; Seneca, *De ira,* 3.2.5. For *D*.50.7.18(17) I would still regard 'law of all peoples' as more likely to be the jurist's meaning. Some historians tend to exaggerate the notion of international law among the Romans: see, e.g., Broughton, "Mistreatment," p. 50.

13. For the episode, see also Cicero, *De oratore,* 1.40.181; 2.32.137; Plutarch, *Tiberius Gracchus,* 7. For a view rather different from that expressed in the text, see H. Lévy-Bruhl, *Quelques problèmes du très ancien droit romain* (Paris, 1934), pp. 43ff.

14. "Hostes sunt, quibus bellum publice populus Romanus decrevit vel ipsi populo Romano: ceteri latrunculi uel praedones appellantur. et ideo qui a latronibus captus est, servus latronum non est, nec postliminium illi necessarium est: ab hostibus autem captus, ut puta a Germanis et Parthis, et servus est hostium et postliminio statum pristinum recuperat."

15. See, e.g., Wissowa, *Religion und Kultus,* pp. 501ff.; Latte, *Religionsgeschichte,* pp. 198ff.

16. But the oath in Roman private law also served purely secular ends: Watson, *State, Law and Religion,* pp. 44ff.

17. Ziegler, "Völkerrecht," p. 70.

18. Watson, *State, Law and Religion.*

## Chapter Six. Breaches of Faith and Manipulation

1. In an oath given by Hannibal to Jupiter and the other gods in 218 B.C., he prayed that if he broke his words the gods would deal with him just as he crushed a lamb's skull with a stone: Livy, 21.45.8. It is agreed that Livy has transferred a Roman ritual to the Carthaginians.

   Probably we should accept that "good faith" was taken seriously in the fetial rites in early times: see, e.g., Tenney Frank, "The Import of the Fetial Institution," *Classical Philosophy* 7 (1912): 335ff.; Ziegler, "Völkerrecht," p. 79.

2. "Lapidem silicem tenebant iuraturi per Iovem, haec verba dicentes: 'Si sciens fallo, tum me Dispiter salva urbe arceque bonis eiciat ut ego hunc lapidem.' "

3. "Hoc demum proelium Samnitium res ita infregit, ut omnibus conciliis fremerent minime id quidem mirum esse, si impio bello et contra foedus suscepto, infestioribus merito deis quam hominibus nihil prospere agerent; expiandum id bellum magna mercede luendumque esse; 11. id. referre tantum, utrum supplicia noxio paucorum an omnium innoxio praebeant sanguine; audebantque iam quidam nominare auctores armorum."

4. Livy, 9.1.

5. "Est autem ius etiam bellicum fidesque iuris iurandi saepe cum hoste servanda. Quod enim ita iuratum est, ut mens conciperet fieri oportere, id servandum est; quod aliter, id si non fecerit, nullum est

periurium. Ut, si praedonibus pactum pro capite pretium non attuleris, nulla fraus sit, ne si iuratus quidem id non feceris; nam pirata non est ex perduellium numero definitus, sed communis hostis omnium; cum hoc nec fides debet nec ius iurandum esse commune. 108. Non enim falsum iurare periurare est, sed, quod EX ANIMI TUI SENTENTIA iuraris, sicut verbis concipitur more nostro, id non facere periurium est. Scite enim Euripides:

Iurávi lingua, méntem iniuratám gero.

Regulus vero non debuit condiciones pactionesque bellicas et hostiles perturbare periurio. Cum iusto enim et legitimo hoste res gerebatur, adversus quem et totum ius fetiale et multa sunt iura communia. Quod ni ita esset, numquam claros viros senatus vinctos hostibus dedidisset." On the text see, e.g., Catalano, *Linee,* 1:4ff.

6. On being commissioned into the U.S. army today, officers swear a similar oath: "I, X, do solemnly swear that I will support and defend the constitution of the United States against all enemies foreign and domestic, that I take this obligation freely without any mental reservation or purpose of evasion."

7. See, e.g., Cicero, *De divinatione,* 2.36.77; cf. Pliny, *Naturalis historia,* 28.4.17.

8. Cicero, *De divinatione,* 1.15.28; 2.34.72–73.

9. See, e.g., Dionysius of Halicarnassus, 4.60.1–61.2.

10. "Tum ubi in coetum Samnitium et ad tribunal ventum Ponti est, A. Cornelius Arvina fetialis ita verba fecit: 'Quandoque hisce homines iniussu populi Romani Quiritium foedus ictum iri spoponderunt atque ob eam rem noxam nocuerunt, ob eam rem quo populus Romanus scelere impio sit solutus hosce homines vobis dedo.' Haec dicenti fetiali Postumius genu femur quanta maxime poterat vi perculit et clara voce ait se Samnitem civem esse, illum legatum a se contra ius gentium violatum: eo iustius bellum gesturos."

11. See the texts in *D.*49.15.

12. Despite the claim, he would not be a Samnite citizen.

*Chapter Seven. Surrender of an Enemy City*

1. Livy, 1.37.5.

2. "Collatia et quidquid citra Collatiam agri erat Sabinis ademptum; Egerius—fratris hic filius erat regis—Collatiae in praesidio relictus. Deditosque Collatinos ita accipio eamque deditionis formulam esse; 2. rex interrogavit: 'Estisne vos legati oratoresque missi a populo Collatino, ut vos populumque Collatinum dederetis?' 'Sumus.' 'Estne populus Collatinus in sua potestate?' 'Est.' 'Deditisne vos populumque Collatinum, urbem, agros, aquam, terminos, delubra, utensilia, divina

humanaque omnia in meam populique Romani dicionem?' 'Dedimus.'
'At ego recipio.' 3. Bello Sabino perfecto Tarquinius triumphans Roman redit."

3. See, above all, Nörr, *Aspekte,* pp. 18ff.

4. Nörr, *Aspekte,* p. 23.

5. C. MARIO     C. FLAVIO [COS.]

   L CAESIO C F IMPERATORE POPULUS SEANO [CORUM SE SUAQUE] DEDIT L
   CAESIUS C F IMPERATOR POSTQUAM [EOS IN FIDEM (DICIONEM?)] ACCEPIT,
   AD CONSILIUM RETOLIT, QUID EIS IM[PERANDUM] CENSERENT DE CONSILI
   SENTENTIA INPERAV[IT ARMA OBSIDES (TRANSFUGAS?)] CAPTIVOS EQUOS
   EQUAS QUAS CEPISENT [UT DEDERENT HAEC] OMNIA DEDERUNT DEINDE EOS
   L CAESIUS C [F IMPERATOR LIBEROS] ESSE IUSSIT, AGROS ET AEDIFICIA LEGES
   CETE[RAQUE OMNIA] QUAE SUA FUISSENT PRIDIE QUAM SE DEDID[ISSENT
   QUAEQUE] EXTARENT EIS REDIDIT, DUM POPULUS [SENATUSQUE] ROMANUS
   VELLET, DEQUE EA RE EOS [ROMAM MITTERE] EIRE IUSSIT LEGATOS. CREN[US
   X. F.] ARCO CANTONI F. LEGATES. Nörr's reconstruction of the missing
   text is placed within square brackets; and his alternative suggestions
   within parentheses.

6. Nörr, *Aspekte,* p. 15. He further suggests that this may be connected
   with the fact that we do not know how a surrender of Rome would
   be carried out.

7. J.-H. Michel is mistaken when he claims that the mechanism of *deditio*
   of a community and of an individual are identical: "Extradition," p.
   675, n.2.

8. See, e.g., W. Dahlheim, *Struktur und Entwicklung des römischen Völker-
   rechts im dritten und zweiten Jahrhundert vor Chr.* (Munich, 1968), pp.
   25ff., 43; Nörr, *Aspekte,* p. 28.

9. "Eadem civitas aliquotiens rebellando semperque adversis contusa
   proeliis tandem se Q. Lutatio consuli dedere coacta est. adversum
   quam saevire cupiens populus Romanus, postquam a Papirio, cuius
   manu iubente consule verba deditionis scripta erant, doctus est Faliscos non potestati, sed fidei se Romanorum conmisisse, omnem iram
   placida mente deposuit."

10. "Nuper M. Claudium ad se nuntium misisse bellum se cum iis, ni
    dederentur, gesturum. 7. Se certam, etsi non speciosam pacem quam
    incerta belli praeoptantes dedidisse se prius in fidem quam in potesta-
    tem populi Romani."

11. See for more detail A. Watson, *Roman Private Law around 200 B.C.*
    (Edinburgh, 1971), p. 60.

12. For the argument see Watson, *Private Law,* pp. 84–85.

13. Livy, 39.54.5–6.

14. Livy, 39.54.11ff. But according to Polybius, 20.9.12, recording events
    of a half century later, to surrender to the faith of the Romans was

equivalent to surrendering to their discretion. I think we have to draw a distinction between theory (where surrender *in fidem* restricted what the Romans could do) and reality (where the Romans could do what they liked). Dieter Nörr, who believes there was only one formulation for the *deditio* of a city, and that is, in effect, that termed *in potestatem*, in which the word *fides* would appear. Still, he holds that *fides* in the surrender was not entirely meaningless, and hypothesizes that the form of surrender developed from the formula for a plebeian entering into the *clientela*, clientship of a patrician: *Die Fides im römischen Völkerrecht* (Heidelberg, 1991), esp. pp. 13ff., 23ff.

15. Cf. Ogilvie, *Livy*, pp. 131–32.
16. Cf. Plutarch, *Numa*, 12.4; quoted in chapter 1.
17. Macrobius, *Saturnalia*, 1.16.22; Cicero, *De divinatione*, 2.36.77; Pliny, *Naturalis historia*, 28.4.17.
18. See, e.g., Livy, 27.25.7ff.; 31.9.5ff.
19. Macrobius, *Saturnalia*, 3.9.9.

*Chapter Eight. Survival and Change*

1. Cf. e.g., Ogilvie, *Livy*, p. 127.
2. "Unum maxime nomen per consensum clamantium Brutuli Papi exaudiebatur. Vir nobilis potensque erat, haud dubie proximarum indutiarum ruptor. 13. De eo coacti referre, praetores decretum fecerunt, ut Brutulus Papius Romanis dederetur et cum eo praeda omnis Romana captivique ut Roman mitterentur, quaeque res per fetiales ex foedere repetitae essent secundum ius fasque restituerentur. 14. Fetiales Romam, ut censuerunt, missi, et corpus Brutuli exanime; ipse morte voluntaria ignominiae se ac supplicio subtraxit. Placuit cum corpore bona quoque eius dedi. 15. Nihil tamen earum rerum praeter captivos ac si qua cognita ex praeda sunt acceptum est; ceterarum rerum inrita fuit deditio. Dictator ex senatus consulto triumphavit."
3. Paradisi uses Livy, 8.39.14 and 9.1.3, as proof that the Samnites had *fetiales*. But in the former text the *fetiales* are Roman, and *fetiales* do not appear in the latter: "Due aspetti," p. 210, n. 81 (at p. 211).
4. For Bellona, see Wissowa, *Religion und Kultus*, pp. 151ff.
5. Livy, 10.19.17; Ovid, *Fasti*, 6.199ff.
6. Cf. Ogilvie, *Livy*, pp. 127–28.
7. "Post tertium autem et tricesimum diem quam res repetissent ab hostibus, fetiales hastam mittebant. denique cum Pyrrhi temporibus adversum transmarinum hostem bellum Romani gesturi essent, nec invenirent locum, ubi hanc sollemnitatem per fetiales indicendi belli celebrarent, dederunt operam, ut unus de Pyrrhi militibus caperetur, quem fecerunt in Circo Flaminio locum emere, ut quasi in hostili loco

ius belli indicendi implerent. denique in eo loco ante aedem Bellonae consecrata est columna. Varro in Caleno ita ait 'duces cum primum hostilem agrum introituri erant, ominis causa prius hastam in eum agrum mittebant, ut castris locum caperent.' "

8. Bellona dicebatur dea bellorum, ante cuius templum erat columella, quae bellica vocabatur, super quam hastam iaciebant, cum bellum indicebatur."

9. Notably, e.g., T. Wiedemann, "The *Fetiales*: A Reconsideration," *Classical Quarterly* 36 (1987): 480ff.

10. Indeed, we must so assume that the fighting was not in accordance with fetial law; otherwise the war would be just, and the captive would have become a Roman slave, and the whole performance would have lost its point.

11. Wiedemann, "The *Fetiales*," p. 481, n. 13. It may be mentioned in passing that there was no prohibition on foreigners buying Roman land, only they could not acquire full ownership. Thus, the land would technically remain Roman.

12. See, e.g., A. Watson, *Failures of the Legal Imagination* (Philadelphia, 1988), pp. 88ff.

13. See Watson, *Failures*, pp. 91ff.

14. See also the example of freeing a slave *vindicta*. In the absence of other ways to the end, a master would have a friend bringing an action against him, claiming that the slave was actually a free man who was wrongfully held. The owner put up no defense, and the slave was adjudged free and a citizen: *G*.3.17. Still, the owner was not held to make restitution for the wrong, he obtained all of a patron's rights over the freedman, and he was owner of everything acquired through the slave—though if the slave had actually been free he would have in some instances acquired ownership for himself.

15. See also W. V. Harris, *War and Imperialism in Republican Rome, 327–70 B.C.* (Oxford, 1979), p. 268.

16. See, e.g., T. Mommsen, *Römisches Staatsrecht*, 3rd ed. (Leipzig, 1887), 2:688ff.; Wissowa, *Religion and Kultus*, p. 554; A. H. McDonald and F. W. Walbank, "The Origins of the Second Macedonian War," *Journal of Roman Studies* 27 (1937): 193.

17. Livy, 21.17.4.

18. "His ita comparatis, ut omnia iusta ante bellum fierent, legatos maiores natu, Q. Fabium M. Livium L. Aemilium C. Licinium Q. Baebium in Africam mittunt ad percunctandos Carthaginienses publicone consilio Hanniba Saguntum oppugnasset."

19. *Bellum Jugurthinum*, 21ff.: see, above all, S. I. Oost, "The Outbreak of the Jugurthine War," *American Journal of Philology* 75 (1954): 147ff.;

cf. D. Timpe, "Herrschaftsidee und Klientalstaatenpolitik in Sallusts Bellum Jugurthinum," *Hermes* 90 (1962): 334ff., esp. 345ff.

20. Cf. Ogilvie, *Livy*, p. 110.

21. "Fetiales, quod fidei publicae inter populos praeerant: nam per hos fiebat ut iustum conciperetur bellum, et inde desitum, ut f⟨o⟩edere fides pacis constitueretur. Ex his mittebantur, ante quam conciperetur, qui res repeterent, et per hos etiam nunc fit foedus, quod fidus Ennius scribit dictum."

22. "Foederum pacis belli indotiarum oratorum fetiales iudices nontii sunto; bella disceptanto." The text has often been regarded as corrupt: cf. an *apparatus criticus*.

23. "Cum regibus foedus in foro i[e]cit porca caesa ac vetere fetialium praefatione adhibita. sed et haec et cetera totumque adeo ex parte magna principatum non tam suo quam uxorum libertorumque arbitrio administravit, talis ubique plerumque, qualem esse eum aut expediret illis aut liberet."

24. "Vixque ubi Grumbates hastam infectam sanguine ritu patrio nostrique more coniecerat fetialis, armis exercitus concrepans, involat muros, confestimque lacrimabilis belli turbo crudescit, rapido turmarum processu, in procinctum alacritate omni tendentium, et contra acri intentaque occursatione nostrorum."

25. Cf. F. de Zulueta, *The Institutes of Gaius* (Oxford, 1953), 2:5.

26. *G*.3.93.

27. "Unde dicitur uno casu hoc verbo peregrinum quoque obligari posse, veluti si imperator noster principem alicuius peregrini populi de pace ita interroget: PACEM FUTURAM SPONDES? vel ipse eodem modo interrogetur. quod nimium subtiliter dictum est, quia, si quid adversus pactionem fiat, non ex stipulatu agitur, sed iure belli res vindicatur."

28. Cf. Catalano, *Linee*, 1:38.

*Chapter Nine. War, Law, and Religion*

1. They did, of course, have political relationships, but no organization in early times. Paradisi, who does use the language of "political organization," points out that he is not referring to any agreement or treaty, but to a "preformed contexture." He also sees a development that was not just a political from a religious base, but a more developed political arrangement from a more backward political arrangement. "Due Aspetti," pp. 189ff.

2. Cf. Saulnier, "Rôle," p. 174.

3. The remarkable nature of the *ius fetiale* is well brought out in Tenney Frank, "The Import of the Fetial Institution," *Classical Philology* 7 (1912): 335ff.

4. "Iniurias et non redditas res ex foedere quae repetitae sint et ego regem nostrum Cluilium causam huiusce esse belli audisse videor nec te dubito, Tulle, eadem prae te ferre; sed si vera potius quam dictu speciosa dicenda sunt, cupido imperii duos cognatos vicinosque populos ad arma stimulat. 8. Neque recte an perperam interpretor; fuerit ista eius deliberatio qui bellum suscepit; me Albani gerendo bello ducem creavere. Illud te, Tulle, monitum velim. Etrusca res quanta circa nos teque maxime sit, quo propior es, hoc magis scis. Multum illi terra, plurimum mari pollent. 9. Memor esto, iam cum signum pugnae dabis, has duas acies spectaculo fore, ut fessos confectosque, simul victorem, ac victum, adgrediantur. Itaque, si nos di amant, quoniam non contenti libertate certa in dubiam imperii servitiique aleam imus, ineamus aliquam viam qua utri utris imperent, sine magna clade, sine multo sanguine utriusque populi decerni possit."

5. On this very basis, the sources that reflect a system working well in very early antiquity, but breaking down or broken down by or before the middle Republic are in harmony with the likely course of events. They provide no support for any thesis that the situation represented for early Rome is a much later invention.

   But in at least the early days, as was argued at the end of Chapter 2, the breakdown would increase the Roman psychological advantage in war.

6. See, e.g., Cicero, *De natura deorum,* 2.3.8; *De harispicum responsis,* 9.19; Sallust, *Bellum Catilinae,* 12.3; *Bellum Jugurthinum,* 14.19; Valerius Maximus, 1.1.8–9; cf., e.g., Wissowa, *Religion und Kultus,* pp. 386ff.; W. H. C. Frend, *Martyrdom and Persecution in the Early Church* (New York, 1967), pp. 77–78.

7. See also, Athenaeus, *Deipnosophistae,* 274a.

8. *De civitate Dei,* 4.8.

9. "Quoniam tamen Romani nominis proprie mentio occurrit, non omittam congressionem, quam provocat illa praesumptio dicentium Romanos pro merito religiositatis diligentissimae in tantum sublimitatis elatos, ut orbem occuparint, et adeo deos esse, ut praeter ceteros floreant qui illis officium praeter ceteros faciant. 3. Scilicet ista merces a Romanis deis pro gratia expensa est. Sterculus et Mutunus et Larentina provexit imperium. Peregrinos enim deos non putem extraneae genti magis fautum voluisse quam suae, et patrium solum, in quo nati, adulti, nobilitati sepultique sunt, transfretanis dedisse."

10. Cf. Marbach, in *RE* 2.3, col. 2412.

11. Cf. K. Vahlert, in *RE* 16.1, cols. 979ff.

12. Ovid, *Fasti,* 3.55ff.; Pliny, *Historia naturalis,* 18.2; Macrobius, *Saturnalia,* 1.10.

13. See, e.g., Dumézil, *Archaic Religion,* 1:32ff.

14. See, e.g., Dumézil, *Archaic Religion*, 1:47ff.; A. Momigliano, in *Cambridge Ancient History*, vol. 7, pt. 2 (Cambridge, 1989), p. 108; Watson, *State, Law and Religion*, pp. 4ff.
15. *De civitate Dei*, 2.4.
16. This paragraph is taken from Watson, *State, Law and Religion*, p. 5.
17. Cf. e.g., Ziegler, "Völkerrecht," p. 79.
18. In *State, Law and Religion* I argue this is the result of putting the interpretation of the Twelve Tables into the control of the College of Pontiffs: pp. 63ff. Although they did not insert religion into secular law, in interpreting that law they used the canons that they were accustomed to use in interpreting sacred law.
19. For other examples, see Watson, *State, Law and Religion*, pp. 65ff.
20. See, e.g., W. Kunkel, *Herkunft und soziale Stellung der römischen Juristen*, 2nd ed. (Graz, 1967), p. 29.
21. "Servus pecuniam ob libertatem pactus erat et eam domino dederat: dominus prius quam eum manumitteret, mortuus erat testamentoque liberum esse iusserat et ei peculium suum legaverat. consulebat, quam pecuniam domino dedisset ob libertatem, an eam sibi heredes patroni reddere deberent necne. respondit, si eam pecuniam dominus, posteaquam accepisset, in suae pecuniae rationem habuisset, statim desisse eius peculii esse: sed si interea, dum eum manumitterent, acceptum servo rettulisset, videri peculii fuisse et debere heredes eam pecuniam manumisso reddere."
22. *Pro Balbo*, 19.45. Of course, Cicero has a lawsuit to argue, so his statement should be treated with reserve.
23. For the connection between Roman religion and war, cf. N. Rosenstein, *Imperatores Victi: Military Defeat and Aristocratic Competition in the Middle and Late Republic* (Berkeley, 1990), pp. 54ff.
24. "Flaminium Caelius religione neglecta cecidisse apud Trasumenum scribit cum magno rei publicae vulnere. Quorum exitio intellegi potest eorum imperiis rem publicam amplificatam qui religionibus paruissent. Et si conferre volumus nostra cum externis, ceteris rebus aut pares aut etiam inferiores reperiemur, religione id est cultu deorum multo superiores."
25. "Aut cum deos esse intellexerit, non intelligat eorum numine hoc tantum imperium esse natum et auctum et retentum?" See also Sallust, *Bellum Catilinae*, 12.3; *Bellum Jugurthinum*, 14.19.
26. 2.72.3. Polybius says that, given the Roman attention to rewards and punishments in the army, it is not surprising that their wars end so brilliantly and successfully: 6.39.11.
27. "7. Q. Fabius Maximus dictator iterum quo die magistratum iniit vocato senatu, ab dis orsus, cum edocuisset patres plus neglegentia caerimoniarum quam temeritate atque inscitia peccatum a C. Flaminio

consule esse quaeque piacula irae deum essent ipsos deos consulendos esse, (8) pervicit ut, quod non ferme decernitur nisi cum taetra prodigia nuntiata sunt, decemviri libros Sibyllinos adire iuberentur. (9) Qui inspectis fatalibus libris rettulerunt patribus, quod eius belli causa votum Marti foret, id non rite factum de integro atque amplius faciundum esse, (10) et Iovi ludos magnos et aedes Veneri Erycinae ac Menti vovendas esse, et supplicationem lectisterniumque habendum, et ver sacrum vovendum si bellatum prospere esset resque publica in eodem quo ante bellum fuisset statu permansisset."

# Index of Texts

## Index of Texts

Varro
  *De lingua latina*
    5.86: 58; 74n.1
    6.88: 16f
Zonaras
    8.7: 87n.7

## Legal Sources

### LAWS

*Duodecim Tabulae*
    2.1b: 80n.35
    2.2: 80n.35
    5.3: 18
    9.3: 80n.35
    12.2a: 36

### INSCRIPTIONS

Alcántara bronze tablet, 49
*C.I.L.*
    1.p.202 el.XLI: 74n.3
    6.913: 76n.32
    6.1302: 75n.16
    6.1497: 76n.32
    6.2059: 84n.6
    8.6987: 76n.32
    14.p.187n.2: 75n.13
*Res gestae divi*
*Augusti*
    7: 76n.33

### PRE-JUSTINIANIAN LEGAL WRITINGS

Gaius
  *Institutiones*
    2.104: 18; 80n.38

    3.17: 92n.14
    3.93: 93n.26
    3.94: 61
    4.13: 79n.22; 80n.8
    4.14: 80n.8
    4.15: 79nn.20, 24
    4.17a: 79n.26; 80n.4
    4.17b: 81n.18
    4.21: 26
    4.73: 23
    4.82: 22
    4.86: 23

### JUSTINIANIAN WORKS

*Digesta*
    1.8.81: 76n.39
    9.3.1.8: 86n.24
    9.4.2.1: 86n.24
    9.4.4pr.: 86n.24
    11.7.36: 80n.16
    30.45.1: 86n.24
    35.2.63pr.: 86n.24
    40.1.6: 67
    48.6.7: 81n.16
    49.15: 80n.5; 89n.11
    49.15.2: 80n.6
    49.15.3: 80n.1
    49.15.24: 41
    50.7.18(17): 41; 81n.16; 87n.12
*Institutiones*
    4.10pr.: 22

# ANCIENT SOCIETY AND HISTORY

The series Ancient Society and History offers books, relatively brief in compass, on selected topics in the history of ancient Greece and Rome, broadly conceived, with a special emphasis on comparative and other nontraditional approaches and methods. The series, which includes both works of synthesis and works of original scholarship, is aimed at the widest possible range of specialist and nonspecialist readers.

*Published in the Series:*
Eva Cantarella, *Pandora's Daughters: The Role and Status of Women in Greek and Roman Antiquity*
Alan Watson, *Roman Slave Law*
John E. Stambaugh, *The Ancient Roman City*
Géza Alföldy, *The Social History of Rome*
Giovanni Comotti, *Music in Greek and Roman Culture*
Christian Habicht, *Cicero the Politician*
Mark Golden, *Children and Childhood in Classical Athens*
Thomas Cole, *The Origins of Rhetoric in Ancient Greece*
Maurizio Bettini, *Anthropology and Roman Culture: Kinship, Time, Images of the Soul*
Suzanne Dixon, *The Roman Family*
Stephen L. Dyson, *Community and Society in Roman Italy*
Tim G. Parkin, *Demography and Roman Society*
Alison Burford, *Land and Labor in the Greek World*
Alan Watson, *International Law in Archaic Rome: War and Religion*